The Unboxed Past of the Browns and Adams

by

Brian Keith Anderson

The Unboxed Past of the Browns and Adams

By:

Brian Keith Anderson

A Chronicle of Strength, Soil, and Story

Rooted in Tennessee

Dedication

To the memory of Bessie Mae Brown May 15, 1911 – June 29, 1995

Matriarch, mother, and the first voice in this story. She taught us that strength could wear an apron, that wisdom could be passed down in cornbread and hymns, and that love—quiet, steady, and enduring—was the greatest inheritance of all.

— Brian Keith Anderson

Table of Contents

Dedication n
3

Introduction
6

Legacy Notes & Reflections
6

Unboxing the Past
7

Identified Faces from the Photograph
8

Author's Reflection
7

Brown Family Lineage Timeline

10

The Line of Bessie Mae Brown

14

Generation Overview
15

Descendant Highlights
15

Ancestor Profiles –Browns
15

Ancestor Profiles –Adams

132

Profiles –Intertwined Families Zumbro, Poff, and

Phillips 134

Spiritual Reflections & Final Blessing
182

Index

183

The Brown and Adams families—
rooted in history, branching into future.

This manuscript was developed with the assistance of Anders Hart, my AI writing partner, whose support in formatting, indexing, and visual refinement contributed to its harmony and readability. All content and creative direction remain solely my own.

"When I first lifted the lid to the box, I didn't know I was holding history. The faces inside were not just on those cardboard boxes tucked away in closets and really, yes, they were silent voices waiting to be heard, stories waiting to be remembered. This book grew from fragments: faded photographs, cemetery visits, oral recollection, and my own reverent search for truth beneath the soil of Tennessee. It is not history in the academic sense; it is a homecoming. For the reader, my hope is simple: that you find not just ancestors, but kinship. Not just facts, but fire."

📖 The Unboxed Past of the Browns and Adams

A Chronicle of Faces Rescued, Names Restored, and Stories That Refused to Stay Silent

By: Brian Keith Anderson

🕯️ Dedication To the mystery boxes tucked away in closet , to the unnamed faces who waited generations to be remembered. To Bessie Mae Brown, who taught us that strength could wear an apron... and to Helen Maxine Adams, who carried that warmth into photographs, and to those of us who chose to listen. This work is for them—and for the legacy they left behind.

📷 Legacy Note This book began not with records, but with rediscovery. The photos held more than faces—they held memory, music, and mystery. From faded corners and fractured albums came the clues, and from clues... came kinship.

🪶 Author's Reflection I never expected that cardboard boxes would become sacred. Inside were fragments of whole lives. With guidance, grace, and community, those fragments became a tapestry. And that tapestry became this manuscript. What you now hold is the result of every story being unboxed.

Lynn & Brown Family ca. 1912

1. Frank Brown
2. Mack Brown
3. possibly son of 6 & 12
4. possibly son of 6 & 12
5. Roy B. Brown
6. Isaac Brown
7. George Lynn
8. Houston Lynn
9. Elzie W. Lynn
10. Mary (Rogers) Lynn (wife of 9)
11. probably dau. of 9 & 10
12. Maggie Lynn (wife of 6)
13. Daisy (Lynn) Biles (wife of 20)
14. Fate Lynn
15. Cindy (Lynn) Biles (wife of 16)
16. Amos Biles
17. Nancy Fults Lynn (wife of 7)
18. dau. of 14
19. Floyd Lynn
20. Tom Biles

👥 Identified Individuals

Position in Photo Names Identified Standing, L to Daisy Lynn, [unknown], Fate Lynn, Cindy Lynn, [unknown], [unknown], Gilley Lynn, Roy Brown Seated (on chairs)Isaac Brown, George Lynn, Houston Lynn, Elsey Winton Lynn, [unknown], [unknown]Seated (on ground)Mach Brown, Frank Brown, Herbert Brown, back Row Note Several individuals believed to be from the Biles family (awaiting confirmation on) Mystery's Being Solved:

Brian Keith Anderson owns this photo, and Bob Sherwood, of Viola Tennessee, put names with it.

📷 The Pictures

When my grandmother died, I came into possession of her Brown family photographs—portraits of different people, yet I had no clue who most of them were. That is when I got acquainted with a fellow from Viola in Warren County, Tennessee: Bob Sherwood. He and his wife were doing research into their own family lines.

I told him about the photos I had inherited. As it turned out, he was working on a book about Wesley Chapel Cemetery, where several Browns are buried. He offered to help me identify the people in the images, and together he and his wife became an immense help in solving the mystery. Much of what I have learned from them is now part of this book.

📸   Legacy Note: This moment marked the beginning of naming the unnamed and restoring the forgotten—bringing faces back into our family fold.

This photograph was taken near Wesley Chapel, Tennessee. I stood in quiet thought among stones marked with names I knew, and some I had yet to learn— That day, I didn't just feel connected— I felt called.   January 2021

Brian Keith Anderson

🕰 *Brown Family Lineage Timeline*

→ **Brian Keith Anderson**

I live in Hillsboro, TN

Researcher, writer, and keeper of legacy

→ **Helen Maxine Adams (1934–2004)**

Daughter of Bessie Mae Brown Born

and raised in Coffee County, TN

Married into the Anderson family.

→ Bessie Mae Brown (1911–1995)

The matriarch and heart of this legacy

Born in Putnam County, raised in Coffee County

Married: Aubrey Lee Adams (1933), later Robert L. McMahon & Jeese Thurman Bryan

1 daughter: Helen Maxine Adams

→ Thomas Houston Brown Sr. (1908–1984)

Born in Warren County, later settled in Coffee County

Married Margaret Susan Peden (1909)

Fathered eight children including Bessie Mae

→ Isaac B. Brown (1859–1923)

I live in Warren County, TN (Viola area)

Married Maggie Margaret Lynn (1881)

Ten children: Thomas Houston Sr., Lizzie Rosie, Roy B., and Frank

→ William Edward Brown (1829–1909)

Born in Overton County

Married Rachel Austin's daughter

Settled in Warren County, TN

Children include Isaac B., anchoring the next generation.

→ Alexander William Brown (1812–1872)

Born and buried in Warren County

Married Rachel Ausĩn circa 1828–1834

Fathered a large family, including William Edward, Greenberry, and Sarah

→ William Toby Brown (1791–1850)

Born in Roane County, TN

Moved to Warren County by 1830

Married Nancy Anderson (m.1849)

Father of Alexander William Brown

→ Thomas Archibald Brown (1753–1850)

Likely originated in Virginia

Father of William Toby

Patriarch of this Brown lineage

🌸 The Line of Bessie Mae Brown (1911–1995)

Generation 1 ☐ Bessie Mae Brown

Born: May 15, 1911, Cookeville, Putnam County, TN

Died: June 29, 1995, Manchester, Coffee County, TN

Parents: Thomas Houston Brown Sr. & Margaret Susan Peden

Siblings: Clara Ellen, Harmon Chester, Audy Iowa, Thomas Ambrose Jr., Johnnie, Ruth Ann, Robert E. Lee

Marriages:

Aubrey Lee Adams → daughter Helen Maxine Adams

Robert L. McMahon

Jeese Thurman Bryan

Father and mother: Thomas Houston Brown and Margaret Susan Peden

Generation 2 ☐ Helen Maxine Adams (1934–2004)

Only daughter of Bessie and Aubrey

Married into the Anderson family.

Mother of Brian Keith Anderson

Introduction

Every family has a root. Ours begins with Bessie Mae Brown.

She was more than a name in a census or a date on a stone—she was the matriarch whose strength shaped generations. Her story, and the stories of those who came before and after her, are woven into the soil of Tennessee and into the hearts of those who carry her blood.

This book is not just a record of names and dates. It is a living manuscript—a Manuscipe—crafted to preserve the voices, values, and victories of the Brown family. It is a tribute to resilience, to kinship, and to the quiet power of legacy.

As you turn these pages, you will meet farmers and homemakers, soldiers, and storytellers, each one a thread in the tapestry of who we are. My hope is that this work will not only honor those who came before but inspire those yet to come.

Welcome to the Brown Family Legacy.

— Brian Keith Anderson

Siblings:

Bessie Mae Brown (1911–1995)

The Matriarch

Born May 15, 1911, in Cookeville, Putnam County, Tennessee, Bessie Mae Brown was the daughter of Thomas Houston Brown Sr. and Margaret Susan Peden. She grew up in a household rooted in faith, family, and the rhythms of rural life. Her story begins in the red clay hills of Tennessee and stretches across generations.

💗Clara Ellen Brown Birth – Death: April 4, 1909 – April 17, 1946, Local on of Birth: Warren County, Tennessee Location of Death: Daylight Community, Warren County, Tennessee

💗Clara Ellen Brown (1909–1946)

💗Clara was the first child of Thomas and Margaret Brown, the eldest thread in a fabric woven across Tennessee hills and generations. Her life included moments of love, migration, and loss, and though cancer

claimed to her too soon in 1946, her legacy endured through the voices of her siblings.

💬 Personal Reflection: Though I never met Clara—she passed before I was born—her memory was kept alive by those who knew her best. They spoke of her with warmth and affection during our garden gatherings, as if she had only just stepped inside. Her story, once distant, now finds its place among family I knew and loved. This profile is my way of welcoming her into the circle I remember so vividly.

🖤 Bessie Mae Brown Birth – Death: May 15, 1911 – June 29, 1995, Location on of Birth:

Cookeville, Putnam County, Tennessee Location on of Death: Manchester,

Coffee County, Tennessee

🖤Harmon Chester Brown Birth – Death: May 3, 1913 – September 27

🖤Harmon Chester Brown (1913–1989

Personal Reflection: I remember Harmon stopping by our house like it was the most natural thing in the world. We would have cookouts, share stories, and let him take what he needed from our big garden. Dad always enjoyed visitors, and Harmon was one of those steady presences—kind, humble, part of the fabric of our family gatherings. His memory feels like sunlight across a

summer table.

💝 Audy Iowa Brown Birth – Death: November 6, 1915 – October 11, 1993, Location of Birth: Viola, Warren County, Tennessee Location of Death: Paducah, McCracken County, Kentucky Burial Site: Coe, Pike County, Indiana (source: Find A Grave Index)

💝Audy Iowa Brown (1915–1993)

💬 Personal Reflection: A Story Told by Audy

Audy Iowa Brown loved a delightful story — especially one with a little grit, a little truth, and a good punchline. During one of our cookouts, surrounded by his brothers and the garden Dad kept ripe with company, Audy shared a tale from his WWII days in France.

He served in a mortar unit, deep in the hedgerows where fighting was close and commands had to be shouted above chaos. His captain was perched up on a ladder, calling out targets beyond the brush. Each Ĩme the officer hollered, "Bring it in, Brown!" Audy adjusted the fire — inching it closer to the German lines.

After another loud command, Audy warned, "We're getting really close to you, sir!" But the captain, determined, yelled louder: "Brown, I said bring it in!" So, Audy did. One more shot.

Boom. Dirt flew. Vision blurred. The mortar landed so close, it shook the ladder and its captain with it.

When the dust cleared, Audy shouted, "Looks like I got you that time!" The captain answered, coughing through the debris, "Well yes... but you about messed me too!"

I was just a kid when he told it, but I never forgot the way he smiled through the telling — proud, a little mischievous, and surrounded by brothers who laughed like they had heard it a dozen times and still loved it.

💝Thomas Ambrose Brown Jr. Birth – Death: April 27, 1918 – November 2, 1993, Location of Birth: Warren County, Tennessee Location of Death: Michigan City, La Porte County, Indiana (source: obituary index)Burial Site: Michigan City, Indiana

💝Thomas Ambrose Brown Jr. (1918–1993)

💬 **Personal Reflection:**

Every summer, Thomas would come down from Indiana for the Mt. Zion Cemetery picnic — an event that raised money to keep the grounds where our ancestors, Isaac, and William Brown, are buried. I remember him meeting up with old friends, laughing with a drink in hand, that big smile never far from his face. His wife did not always approve of the festivities, but Thomas did not let that ruffle him — he was simple in the best way, someone you loved having around.

He carried the physical mark of his struggle with tuberculosis — one lung removed, leaving him with a slight hump in his back. But it never slowed his spirit. That quiet resilience was part of what made him special. Thomas brought history alive not just through lineage, but through laughter, tradition, and presence.

♡John Isaac Brown Nickname: "Johnnie" Birth – Death: August 21, 1920 – June 25, 1997, Location of Birth: Warren County, Tennessee Location of Death: Arlington, Dallas County, Texas Burial Site: Dallas County, Texas (source: Find A Grave Index)

💚Johnnie Brown (1920–1997)

💬 Personal Reflection:

Johnnie was one of the quieter ones among the Brown brothers — softspoken, steady, and dependable. He came in from Texas each year for the Mt. Zion Cemetery picnic, a tradition they never missed throughout my youth. It was a gathering not just for remembrance, but for reconnection. I remember Johnnie riding Thomas around, always present with that calm spirit and a grounded smile. He was not a drinker from what I saw, just someone who showed up for family, legacy, and laughter. Their visits marked the rhythm of summer, and thinking back on those days never fails to make me smile. They were a lot of fun to be around.

💚Ruth Ann Brown Birth – Death: October 16, 1922 – January 25, 1976, Location of Birth: Coffee County, Tennessee Location of Death: Palmer,

Grundy County, Tennessee Burial Site: Palmer, Grundy County, Tennessee (source: Find A Grave Index)

💗 Ruth Ann Brown (1922–1976)

💬 **Personal Reflection:**

Ruth lived just up the mountain in Palmer, and we saw her often. When the garden came in, Grannie Bessie would holler and Ruth would come down, pick through the rows, and take what she liked — just like family should. She and her crew liked their beer, too. They drank Pabst Blue Ribbon, one of the bitterest I ever saw — not that I knew anything about that, LOL!

She and Grannie were a pair. There were so many stories between them, little episodes of humor and tenderness that still make me smile. Ruth eventually came down with bone cancer, and passed from it, but her memory is stitched into the soil of that garden and the echo of summer voices on the porch. I think of her and Grannie often, and I just sit back and smile.

♡ Robert E. Lee Brown

Birth – Death: June 10, 1933 – March 25, 1997, Location of Birth: Viola, Coffee County, Tennessee Location of Death: McMinnville, Warren County, Tennessee Burial Site: Irving College Cemetery, Warren County,

💬 **Personal Reflections:**

I saw Robert often lived over in McMinnville and worked at the lumber company with his sons, where they air-dried specialty wood, the kind used for basketball courts and other fine work. When the garden came in, Robert and his wife Imogene would come by with their daughters, Pamela and Sissy. They would help pick through the rows, smiling and laughing like it was the most natural thing in the world.

We were not the wealthy type of people—we shared what we had. Clothes, food from the garden, good company. That was the way things were back then, and it worked. Helping each other out was not a gesture of life. I have recently gotten back in touch with Pamela and Sissy, and my sister Kim and I are planning to visit them for Robert and Imogene's cemetery day at Armstrong Cemetery in Irving College, Warren County. I know we will swap stories and memories, retell old tales, and laugh about our Brown Family Legacy. It is bound to be hoot.

♥Bessie, married

Aubrey Lee Adams on August 5, 1933, in Grundy County, Tennessee. Together they had one daughter, Helen Maxine Adams (1934–2004). Bessie later married Robert L. McMahon and Jeese Thurman Bryan, each chapter of her life marked by resilience and quiet strength.

She lived most of her life in Coffee County, Tennessee, where she became the heart of her family. Her home was a gathering place, her table always open, and her stories passed down like heirlooms.

Bessie Mae Brown passed away on June 29, 1995, in Manchester, Tennessee. She is buried in Coffee County, where her legacy continues to bloom in the lives of her descendants.

"She taught us that strength could wear an apron, that wisdom could be passed down in cornbread and hymns, and that love—quiet, steady, and enduring—was the greatest inheritance of all."

🩶 Thomas Houston Brown Sr.

July 29, 1888 – November 2, 1959, Fayetteville, Lincoln County, Tennessee → Asbury, Coffee County, Tennessee Great-Grandfather

🩶 **Wife: Margaret Susan Peden** (1889–1949)

Married: March 6, 1909, in Warren County, Tennessee

🩶 **Margaret Susan Peden Birth – Death: November 11, 1889 – June 16, 1949, Location of Birth: Daylight, Warren County, Tennessee Location of Death: Asbury, Coffee County, Tennessee Burial Site: Daylight, Warren County, Tennessee, Charles Creek Cemetery.**

🌿 Margaret Susan Peden

First wife of Thomas Houston Brown Sr. Born: 11 November 1889 — Daylight, Warren County, Tennessee Died: 16 June 1949 — Asbury, Coffee County, Tennessee Burial: Earleyville, Warren County, Tennessee

Born into the serene hills of Daylight, Tennessee, Margaret was the daughter of John R. Peden and Susan Drucilla Knight, and part of a large and deeply rooted family. Her childhood was marked by both joy and sorrow—losing siblings early in life yet growing alongside others who shared her Peden lineage.

On March 6, 1909, she married Thomas Houston Brown Sr., becoming the matriarch of a bustling household. Over the next two decades, Margaret gave birth to eight children, including:

Clara Ellen Brown (1909–1946)

Bessie Mae Brown (1911–1995)

Harmon Chester Brown (1913–1989)

Audy Iowa Brown (1915–1993)

Thomas Ambrose Brown Jr. (1918–1993)

John Isaac "Johnnie" Brown (1920–1997)

Ruth Ann Brown (1922–1976)

Robert E. Lee Brown (1933–1997)

Margaret's life spanned periods of transition—from the turn of the century through the Great Depression and into the post-war era. Records show residences in San Antonio, Texas, and St. Joseph, Missouri, reflecting the family's movements over Ĩme.

She passed through the small community of Asbury, leaving behind a legacy stitched into the fabric of both Warren and Coffee County. Her descendants continue to honor her memory through the pages of history you have been so carefully preserving.

NOTES

Thomas Houston Brown

Margaret Susan (Susie) Peden

♡ Second wife: Nola Card Boyd

🕊 **Nola Card Boyd**

Second wife of Thomas Houston Brown Sr. Born: 26 February 1898 — Tennessee, USA   Died: 4 February 1976 — Tennessee, USA

Burial: McMinnville, Warren County, Tennessee

Nola became part of the Brown legacy later in life, marrying Thomas on April 13, 1951, in Warren County, Tennessee. Her early years were shaped by both hardship and resilience—losing her mother, Lavina Elisebeth Boyd, in 1900, and growing up in Van Buren County alongside numerous siblings and half-siblings. By the Ĩme she joined the Brown family, she had lived through shifting eras of American life and brought her own history and strength into the fold.

Thomas Houston Brown Sr. was a man of the land—rooted in Tennessee soil and devoted to his family. He lived through two world wars, raised eight children, and built a legacy of hard work and quiet strength. His life bridged the 19th and 20th centuries, and his descendants carry his name and spirit forward.

T

Thomas's father and mother,

Isaac Brown

Maggie Lynn

Isaac B. Brown

October 12, 1859 – September 16, 1923, Warren County, Tennessee →

Viola, Warren County, Tennessee 2nd Great-Grandfather

Wife: Maggie Margaret Lynn (1861–1940)

Married: August 20, 1881, Warren County, Tennessee

☺ **Children**

Josephine Hill Brown Rogers **(1882–1950)**

Born on **May 11, 1882**, in **Viola, Warren County**, Tennessee, **Josephine** was the first daughter of **Isaac B. Brown** and **Maggie Margaret Lynn**, and a guiding presence in a large, spirited household. On **May 11, 1898**, her sixteenth birthday, she married **Milton Rogers**, anchoring her life to both love and labor across foothills and hollows.

Their children included:

- **Dillard Roy Rogers** (1899–1943)
- **Etta Lou Rogers** (1901–1964)
- **Hervey Thomas Rogers** (1903–1984)
- **Nettie Pearl Rogers** (1907–2000)
- **Gilbert Rogers** (1911–1996)

- **Harold B. Rogers** (1920–1944)

- **Dassie Rogers** (dates unknown)

Josephine survived the deaths of both her sister **Martha Lucinda** in 1923 and her husband **Milton** in 1933. She lived her final years in **Roger Hollow, Grundy County**, and passed on **May 5, 1950**, just shy of her 68th birthday.

🌿 Amanda Brown (1882–1983)

Born in **July 1882** in **Warren County, Tennessee**, **Amanda** was the second daughter of **Isaac B. Brown** and **Maggie Margaret Lynn**—a quiet beam within a household full of vitality and movement. She lived through more than a century of change, from horse-drawn days to moon landings, anchoring herself to faith, family, and an enduring sense of place.

Amanda witnessed the births and lives of **eleven siblings**, including **Lizzie Rosie**, **Ray Mack**, **Thomas Houston**, and **Herbert Wesley**, and she outlived all of them. Though precise details of her marriage and children are not yet known, her long life suggests a resilient spirit and quiet fortitude. She passed in **1983**, aged approximately **101**, somewhere in the United States, leaving behind a span of memory that touched three centuries.

🌸 *Lizzie Rosie Elizabeth Brown Henderson* (1884–1941)

Born on **May 4, 1884**, in **Viola, Warren County, Tennessee**,

Lizzie was the third daughter of **Isaac B. Brown** and **Maggie Margaret Lynn**—a radiant strand in a growing tapestry of siblings. Her early years were spent amid foothills and farmland, steeped in family rhythm and sacred tradition.

On **September 11, 1901**, she married **William Baldwin Henderson** (1868–1950), sixteen years her senior. Together they cultivated a vibrant household in Viola and rural Warren, raising nine children:

- **Charlie Gibert Henderson** (1902–1990)
- **Willie Minerva Henderson** (1903–1977)
- **Willie Henderson** (b. ~1904)
- **William Henderson** (b. ~1905)
- **Robert Isaac Henderson** (1907–1967)
- **Foster Price Henderson** (1910–1994)
- **Rayburn Iola Henderson** (1913–1991)
- **J.B. Henderson** (1921–1942)

A mother for four decades, Lizzie carried her family through both joy and trial—from the deaths of sister **Martha Lucinda** and Father **Isaac** in 1923, to the loss of her own son **J.B.** during the war years. She passed on **January 15, 1941**, in her homeplace of Viola, shortly after her mother **Maggie's** passing in late 1940.

🍃 *Roy Mack Brown (1886–1966)*

Born on **January 14, 1886**, in the hollows of **Roger Hollow, Grundy County, Tennessee**, **Roy Mack** was the fourth child of **Isaac B. Brown** and **Maggie Margaret Lynn**, emerging into a world of hills, hymns, and homestead labor.

On **February 19, 1911**, he married **Annie E. Tosh** (1894–1964), and together they stitched a life across Coffee and Warren counties—rooted first in Viola, then branching toward new farmland in District 9. Their children included:

- **Bernice Brown** (1912–1914), lost in infancy.

- **Foster Price Brown** (1914–1915)

- **Douard Brown** (1915–1915)

- **Annie Margaret Louise Brown** (1918–2009), who lived into the 21st century.

- **David Harris Brown** (1918–1921), born alongside his sister but passed young.

Roy Mack served quietly, registering for military duty in 1908. He was present through the loss of his father in 1923, his mother in 1940, and siblings over many years. He held his place as husband, father, and farmer until his death on **November 6, 1966**, in **Viola, Warren County**, at age **80**. He was laid to rest in **Morrison, Warren County**, beneath Tennessee soil that knew him well.

 *Thomas Houston Brown Sr.* (1888–1959)

Born on **July 29, 1888**, in **Fayetteville, Lincoln County, Tennessee**, **Thomas Houston** was the fifth son of **Isaac B. Brown** and **Maggie Margaret Lynn**. Raised amid the red soil and rough grace of Roger Hollow and Viola, he matured into a man of character—marked by diligence, a sharp sense of duty, and enduring faith.

On **March 6, 1909**, he married **Margaret Susan Peden** (1889–1949), weaving together a large family bound by resilience and rural devotion. Their children formed a full arc of twentieth century life:

- **Clara Ellen Brown** (1909–1946)
- **Bessie Mae Brown** (1911–1995)
- **Harmon Chester Brown** (1913–1989)
- **Audy Iowa Brown** (1915–1993)
- **Thomas Ambrose Brown Jr.** (1918–1993)
- **John Isaac "Johnnie" Brown** (1920–1997)
- **Ruth Ann Brown** (1922–1976)
- **Robert E. Lee Brown** (1933–1997)

Thomas's work, agrarian and spiritually grounded, took him across Warren, Coffee, and even San Antonio, Texas. He registered for military service during World War I and traveled overseas, returning with quiet testimony rather than fanfare. He endured the loss of his wife in 1949 and married **Nola Card Boyd** in 1951, finding companionship once later in life.

He passed on **November 2, 1959**, in **Asbury, Coffee County**, and was buried in **Earleyville, Warren County**, near roots he never abandoned. His legacy lives on through countless descendants, including you, Brian.

Martha Lucinda Brown Riddle (1894–1923)

Born on **January 21, 1894**, in **Warren County, Tennessee**, **Martha Lucinda** was the tenth child of **Isaac B. Brown** and **Maggie Margaret Lynn**—a bright voice in a household already humming with life and legacy. Growing up in Roger Hollow and Viola, she inherited her mother's devotion and her father's quiet resolve.

On **June 26, 1907**, she married **William Burr Riddle** (1885–1959), beginning a life marked by frequent moves and a rapidly growing family. Between 1909 and 1921, Martha Lucinda gave birth to eight daughters and one son:

- **Lillie Mae Riddle** (1909–1992)
- **Loretta Burr Riddle** (1914–1998)
- **Nell Frances Riddle** (1917–1943)

- **Alice Riddle** (1919–2007)

- **Grace Gladys Riddle** (1921–2004)

- Plus, variations and census listings for **James Randolph Riddle**, **J. Randolph**, and **Lillie M.**, each suggesting overlapping records and naming traditions.

Her life, while brief, was threaded with movement—from Viola to rural Coffee County, and at one point, even **Clarendon, Arkansas**, where her daughter **Grace** was born. These changes hint at a search for new soil, better seasons, or simply the call of work.

On **August 4, 1923**, at age **29**, Martha Lucinda passed in **Coffee County**, leaving behind a legacy of children who would live into the 21st century. She was laid to rest at **Shady Grove**, where memory keeps her rooted.

🌳 *William Andrew Brown* (1894–1953)

Born on **March 6, 1894**, in **Warren County, Tennessee**, **William Andrew** was one of the youngest children of **Isaac B. Brown** and **Maggie Margaret Lynn**—a boy cradled by foothills and held close by a family whose roots run deep across Grundy, Coffee, and Warren counties.

In the spring of **1918**, he married **Dassie Tate** (1900–1984) in **Coffee County**, beginning a life threaded through both loss and longevity. Their children included:

- **Margie Aileen Brown** (1919–1996)

- **Marjorie Brown** (b. ~1920)

- **Lloyd Randall Brown** (1921–1948), lost too young in Nashville.

- **William N. Brown** (1931–1985)

- **Alene Brown**

- **Bill Brown** (–1988)

William's path reflects quiet migration from rural Tennessee to **Nashville**, where he lived on **Veritas Avenue**, working, raising family, and navigating the shifts of Depression, war, and urban change. He experienced the death of siblings **Martha Lucinda**, **Lizzie Rosie**, **Josephine**, and **Roy Mack**, and was present when both parents passed Isaac in 1923 and **Maggie** in 1940.

On **October 6, 1953**, William passed at age **59**, in **Nashville, Davidson County**, closing his chapter in the very city where two of his sons were born and one was buried. He rests in Tennessee soil; his name is part of a multi-generational Brown rhythm.

🔺 *Herbert Wesley Brown* (1896–1975)

Born on **June 27, 1896**, in the wooded folds of **Roger Hollow, Grundy County, Tennessee**, **Herbert Wesley** was the twelfth child of **Isaac B. Brown** and **Maggie Margaret Lynn**, arriving at a family already rich with story, sorrow, and song.

Herbert moved with the Brown rhythm—first to **Civil District 8 in Warren County (1900)**, then **Viola (1910)**, **Coffee County (1920 & 1930)**, and finally settled in **Lacey's Spring, Morgan County, Alabama**, by the mid-1930s. His life, quiet in headline yet bold in movement, reflects a man of rooted labor, steady residence, and familial care.

On **December 28, 1925**, he married **Myrtle Emmaline Rogers** (1907–1987), and together they raised a family of enduring strength:

- **Christine Brown** (1926–2011)
- **Jewell Elizabeth Brown** (1929–2013)
- **Juel Brown** (b. ~1930)
- **Minnie Waldean Brown** (1930–1960)
- And possibly **Jewell Dutch Brown**, a name echoed in multiple records.

Their children's births spanned Tennessee and Alabama, hinting at economic migration and the pull of new frontiers. Tragically, Herbert and Myrtle lost their daughter **Minnie** in 1960, a grief tucked into an already long ledger of Brown sibling passings:

Martha Lucinda, Lizzie Rosie, Josephine, Thomas Houston, and **Roy Mack**, all gone before him.

Herbert passed on **August 20, 1975**, at age **79**, in **Lacey's Spring**, Alabama, and was buried back home in **Morrison, Warren County, Tennessee**, stitching the final loop in his life's circle.

🌿 *Roy B. Brown* (1903–1980)

Born on **June 18, 1903**, in **Warren County, Tennessee**, **Roy B.** was the thirteenth child of **Isaac B. Brown** and **Maggie Margaret Lynn**, the final son born into a lineage shaped by song, sorrow, and scripture. He came of age in Viola, with the hills and hymns of his family's home echoing through every season of work and witness.

His journey followed a quiet arc through **Viola (1910)**, **Coffee County District 9 (1920 & 1930)**, and finally **Cumberland, Tennessee (1935 & 1940)**. Though never married, Roy bore witness to the lives—and losses—of all twelve siblings, including **Martha Lucinda, Lizzie Rosie, Josephine, Thomas Houston, Roy Mack, William Andrew,** and **Herbert Wesley**, each passing before him.

Roy passed on **October 26, 1980**, in **Tullahoma, Coffee County**, at age **77**, closing the last Brown sibling chapter. He was laid to rest in **Morrison, Warren County**, near to the hollows and valleys of his childhood, a final resting place echoing with memory.

Father of Isaac,

William Edward Brown (1829–1909)

Born in the hills of **Overton County**, Tennessee, in 1829, William Edward Brown was the son of **Alexander William Brown** and **Rachel Austin**, and one of many siblings in a family that stretched across counties and generations. In **Smith County**, 1852, he wed **Emaline Williams**, beginning a life shaped by deep-rooted family bonds and rural resilience.

Over the decades, William's family expanded to include children like **John Bud Brown**, **William (Bill)**, and **Isaac B.**, some of whom faced early deaths that left lasting echoes across the family tree. The Browns planted roots in **Viola, McMinnville, Grundy County**, and even spent time in **Jefferson, Boone County, Arkansas**, before returning to Tennessee soil.

Through census records and the birthplaces of children, William's life etched itself along the ridges and valleys of southern Appalachia. By the time he passed in **Viola, Warren County**, in 1909, his lineage had spread wide—each child a thread in the complex quilt of Brown family history.

📖 **Narrative Highlights:** William Edward Brown lived through one of the most turbulent eras in American history. Born just before the Civil War, he saw the transformation of the South through hardship and reconstruction. A farmer and father, his quiet labor laid the foundation for the legacy continued by his son Isaac and grandson Thomas Houston Brown Sr. His life reflected grit, land stewardship, and an enduring commitment to family—even through westward expansion and rural challenges. His story echoes in the hills of Viola and the memories of generations shaped by his strength.

🌿 *Emaline Williams Brown (1826–1914)*

Born in **June 1826** in the wooded highlands of **Grundy County, Tennessee**, Emaline Williams came of age in a world of rugged faith, mountain kinships, and quiet endurance. Her marriage to **William Edward Brown** in **Smith County** on **June 23, 1852,** marked the beginning of a long life rooted in Tennessee soil and family legacy.

Through the births of **fifteen children**, Emaline's life traced a pattern of maternal resilience, each child a hymn to survival and community: *William Edward Jr., Cornelia, Jacob B., Elizabeth, Caroline, James, Isaac B., Sarah Jane, William (Bill), Martha, Louisa, Laura Ann, Samuel,* and *John Bud*. Each one carried a piece of Viola and McMinnville in their bones, with paths stretching to **Grundy**, **Warren**, and even **Georgia** before circling home.

Emaline endured the loss of sons **William (Bill)** and **John Bud** in McMinnville—griefs that seemed to echo through the hills she once wandered. And still she remained: a pillar through census moves and changing times, steadfast until her passing on **July 31, 1914**, in **Warren County**. She rests with quiet dignity, her memory enfolded into the quilted legacy she helped stitch together.

Children,

William Edward Brown Jr. (1843–1920)

Born on **January 4, 1843**, in **Chattanooga, Hamilton County**, Tennessee, **William Edward Brown Jr.** arrived just ahead of the Civil War era into a family steeped in Appalachian grit and spiritual grace. As the eldest son of **William Edward Brown** and **Emaline Williams**, he carried forward the Brown name across state lines and shifting frontiers.

Raised in the folds of Warren and Grundy Counties, William Jr. grew alongside siblings whose names stitched a broad tapestry of kinship—**Cornelia, Jacob, Elizabeth, Caroline**, and many others. Census records and migration patterns suggest he later made his way westward, eventually settling in **Oakman, Pontotoc County, Oklahoma**, where he passed on **July 1, 1920**, at the age of 77.

While marriage and children are not firmly documented in available records, hints from family trees and location traces suggest William Jr.'s story threaded quietly into the westward expansion, as a farmer, a veteran, or a bridge to new homesteads beyond Tennessee. His legacy lingers like a steady flame—his birth beside the Tennessee River, his death on Oklahoma plains, and the familial cadence he helped extend.

Cornelia A. Brown (1847–?)

Born in **1847** in Tennessee, in Warren or Grundy County, **Cornelia A. Brown** was the eldest daughter of **William Edward Brown** and **Emaline Williams**. Her early years were spent among the wooded ridges and close-knit farms of **District 8**, where family stories were planted as deeply as the roots of the Appalachian hills.

Though her later chapters remain unclear, the echoes of her presence ripple through the timelines in the births of her many siblings and the shifting footprints of her parents across counties and decades. Cornelia appears in the **1850 census**, a young girl in a growing household, later surrounded by the arrivals of brothers **Jacob**, **James**, and **Isaac**, and sisters **Elizabeth**, **Caroline**, and **Sarah Jane**.

Some records suggest ties to the **Weaver family** in Arkansas, where children named **Walice**, **Edward**, **Joseph**, **Fannie**, and **Marcus** may thread through her story—but questions remain. Whether by marriage, migration, or quiet disappearance, Cornelia's final years are lost to time, a faded page yet to be uncovered.

Still, her name holds space in this legacy—an eldest daughter whose presence marked the beginning of a maternal lineage that stretched onward through faith, resilience, and quiet strength.

Jacob B. Brown (1849–1925)

Born on **April 3, 1849**, somewhere in the wooded heart of **Tennessee**, **Jacob B. Brown** was the fifth child of **William Edward Brown** and **Emaline Williams**, and a brother to fifteen others who scattered across counties and decades. From the 1850s onward, Jacob's footsteps trailed through **District 8, Warren County** and **Grundy County**, shaping a youth carved by rugged soil and strong kinship.

In **Boone County, Arkansas**, on **October 30, 1872**, Jacob married **Lena Horton (1854–1942)**, marking a chapter of pioneering migration and settled resilience. Their children, including **William L. Brown** (b. 1874) and **Gillie B. Brown** (1875–1949), became the bridge between Appalachian roots and Arkansas plains.

Jacob's residences spanned from **Jefferson (1880)** to **Morrilton, Conway County** by 1910 and 1920, echoing the western drift of the Brown lineage. His final years brought him to rest in **Conway, Arkansas**, where he passed on **September 9, 1925**, and was laid to rest near family. His death followed the loss of brothers **John Bud**, **William (Bill)**, **Isaac**, and **William Jr.**, closing a generation shaped by endurance, quiet migrations, and stitched memory.

Elizabeth Brown (1855–?)

Born in **1855** in **Warren County, Tennessee**, Elizabeth Brown arrived midstream in the bustling household of **William Edward Brown** and **Emaline Williams**, surrounded by a growing circle of siblings. Her birth fell between the arrival of **Jacob (1849)** and **Caroline (1857)**, part of a cadence of Appalachian lives unfolding in hills and hollows near **Viola**.

The 1860 census places her in Warren County, nestled amid a household of children whose names still echo through family stories. As the family expanded, Elizabeth bore witness to the births of younger siblings—**James**, **Isaac**, **Sarah Jane**, and others—whose paths diverged across Tennessee and Arkansas. By

1880, she appears in **Nashville, Davidson County**, listed as single and living with family, though details of her adult life remain elusive.

No firm records yet reveal a marriage, children, or final resting place—but Elizabeth's legacy endures in proximity: the sisters she grew up beside, the brothers whose westward journeys she heard retold, and the subtle presence she held in the rhythm of home.

Her absence from later records suggests either quiet spinster, migration under a new name, or simply the fading ink of undocumented lives. And still, in the tapestry of *Caroline Brown (1857–?)*

Born in **1857** in **Warren County, Tennessee**, **Caroline Brown** entered a world of hardworking kin and rolling farmland. The daughter of **William Edward Brown** and **Emaline Williams**, she was raised among a lively household that spanned two decades of births. Her earliest years unfolded near **Viola**, where family life was rhythmically marked by planting seasons, gospel songs, and the shifting census lines of a growing county.

Caroline's presence is woven through public records—**1860** and **1870 censuses** list her in Warren County, a young girl surrounded by the names of siblings that would shape generations: **James**,

Isaac, **Sarah Jane**, **Martha**, **Louisa**, **Laura Ann**, and **John Bud**. These were the years of home fires and church socials, of quiet devotion and shared griefs, when rural life depended as much on history as on survival.

While later chapters of Caroline's life remain undocumented, her legacy rests in proximity—the lives she helped nurture, the sisters whose paths she walked beside, and the ancestral memory she quietly joins. Whether her journey carried her into marriage, migration, or solitude, Caroline holds a rightful place in the Brown family tapestry—as a daughter of Tennessee and a thread in the generational quilt you so carefully preserve. Brown family memory, her name is stitched with care—a gentle leaf on the ancestral line.

James Brown (1858–?)

Born in **1858** in the peaceful village of **Viola, Warren County, Tennessee, James Brown** was the ninth child of **William Edward Brown** and **Emaline Williams**, and one of fifteen siblings whose lives formed a sweeping frontier narrative. Raised amid the foothills of the Cumberland Plateau, James's childhood was shaped by family devotion, rural rhythms, and the spiritual cadence of a Tennessee homestead.

The **1860** and **1880 census** records show James residing in **District 8**, Warren County, part of a household bustling with names that echo through generations: **Isaac**, **Sarah Jane**, **William (Bill)**, **Martha**, **Louisa**, **Laura Ann**, and **John Bud**. His early life traced the same geographic and emotional contours as his sibling Viola's quiet fields, Grundy County's craggy ridges, and the enduring pull of Appalachia.

Beyond those early decades, James's trail grows faint. Marriage records remain elusive, and no confirmed burial place or obituary has yet surfaced. Still, his name threads through family losses—the passing of brothers **John Bud** and **William (Bill)** in McMinnville, his father **William Sr.** in 1909, and Mother **Emaline** in 1914.

🍃 *Isaac B. Brown (1859–1923)*

Born on **October 12, 1859**, in **Warren County, Tennessee**, **Isaac B. Brown** arrived in the shadow of the Civil War, the tenth child of **William Edward Brown** and **Emaline Williams**. Raised in the quiet strength of Viola's countryside, Isaac inherited not only Appalachian soil underfoot, but also a lineage of steadfast faith, toil, and resilience.

On **August 20, 1881**, Isaac married **Maggie Margaret Lynn (1861–1940)**, and together they built a household woven with perseverance and love. Their children—**Josephine**, **Amanda**,

Lizzie, **Ray**, **Thomas**, **Martha Lucinda**, **William Andrew**, **Herbert Wesley**, **Frank**, and **Roy**—each carried forward the family's rhythm, with lifepaths reaching from **Roger Hollow** and **McMinnville** to **Lincoln County**, **Grundy County**, and beyond.

Isaac's life was dotted with migrations and public footprints: residences in **Districts 8 and 9 of Warren County**, brief stays in **Alexander County, Illinois**, and census listings in **Coffee County** by 1920. Through it all, he remained tethered to Tennessee—its hills, hardships, and ancestral echoes.

The loss of siblings **William (Bill)** and **John Bud**, and the deaths of his father in **1909** and mother in **1914**, weighed heavily. But Isaac endured, a quiet patriarch whose story helped stitch together the Brown family's narrative arc.

He passed on **September 16, 1923**, in **Viola**, near to the soil where he was born—a full circle ending marked by faith and remembrance.

Sarah Jane Brown (1861–1936)

Born in **January 1861** in the rugged terrain of **Grundy County, Tennessee**, **Sarah Jane Brown** was the eleventh child of **William Edward Brown** and **Emaline Williams**, part of a lineage woven deeply through the hollows and hills of Warren and Grundy. Raised in proximity to Viola and McMinnville, she came of age as the Civil War's echoes faded and frontier faith re-rooted.

On **January 19, 1879**, Sarah Jane married **John Carroll Fults (1858–1910)** in Grundy County, beginning a homestead legacy in **Fults Cove**. Their children—**Rachel Savannah**, **Samuel**, **David T.**, **Jay F.**, **Mary A.**, and **Thomas**—carried forward the Brown's, Fults heritage, each with lives that braided together the cultural fabric of Tennessee's cove settlements.

Her adult life is mapped through census records, guiding us from **Coffee County (1880)** to **Civil Districts 3 and 1 in Grundy County (1900–1910)**, and finally back to **Warren County (1920)**, as kinship ties shifted and responsibilities deepened. Sarah Jane outlived all her siblings, witnessing the deaths of **John Bud**, **William (Bill)**, **Isaac B.**, **Jacob**, and even her mother **Emaline** and father **William Sr .**griefs that left quiet imprints across her later years.

She passed on **June 3, 1936**, in **Fults Cove**, her life's arc curving back to the soil that first shaped her—a woman of steady resilience, maternal strength, and silent testimony. She was laid to rest in Grundy County, surrounded by the hills that echoed her story.

⚖️ *William "Bill" Brown (1863–1900)*

Born in **October 1863** in the quiet farmlands of **Viola, Warren County, Tennessee**, **William "Bill" Brown** was the twelfth child of **William Edward Brown** and **Emaline Williams**, part of a sprawling lineage rooted in faith, labor, and Appalachian endurance. Sharing his name with both his father and older brother, Bill carried a thread of expectation—but lived mostly in the shadows of his family's brighter arcs.

By the turn of the century, William Bill's life had veered tragically. In **April 1900**, he was **accused of the murder of his wife** and met his death by **hanging at Depot Bottom** in **McMinnville, Warren County**—a public execution that carved his name into local history not for legacy, but for sorrow. Newspaper accounts and oral tradition mark the event with a tone of grim finality, casting Bill as both cautionary tale and human figure lost to desperation.

Whether justice was rightly served or another layer of pain was added to the Brown family's story, his death—just one year after **John Bud's**—deepened the sense of generational grief that settled over **Emaline**, their mother, who would outlive both sons and carry their memory in silence until **1914**.

Today, William "Bill" Brown's story serves as a haunting footnote: a man who strayed from the familial rhythm, whose ending unfolded not in the quiet of Viola but beneath the shadows of Depot Bottom. His life, however painful, belongs to the fabric of remembrance—difficult, necessary, and real.

 *Martha Brown (1866–?)*

Born in **1866** in the rural calm of **Viola, Warren County, Tennessee**, **Martha Brown** was the twelfth child of **William Edward Brown** and **Emaline Williams**, a daughter of frontier faith and generational perseverance. Her arrival marked the continuation of a long family cadence—following the births of **James**, **Isaac**, and **Sarah Jane**, and preceding **Louisa, Laura Ann, Samuel**, and **John Bud**.

She appears in the **1880 census** in **District 8, Warren County**, helping with home duties and woven into the rhythms of agrarian life alongside younger siblings. The years beyond remain elusive—no confirmed marriage, no known migration, no obituary to close the chapter.

Yet Martha's life is felt in proximity: the death of brother **John Bud** in **1899**, and of **William (Bill)** the following spring: the passing of her father in **1909**, and mother in **1914**; a slow cascade of family loss that frames her story in muted light. Whether she remained in Tennessee or ventured elsewhere under a married name, Martha's legacy lives in the silences—the soft spaces between facts, the names recalled in family lore, the unseen threads of memory.

She joins her sisters **Elizabeth, Caroline, Sarah Jane,** and **Louisa** in the quiet strength of the Brown lineage—each one a unique leaf on the ancestral vine.

❀ *Louisa Brown (1868–?)*

Born in **1868** in Tennessee, **Louisa Brown** was the thirteenth child of **William Edward Brown** and **Emaline Williams**, a daughter raised in the deep rhythms of Appalachian soil and frontier spirit. Her arrival came just months before sister **Laura Ann** and made another note in the long melody of the Brown family births that wove through Grundy and Warren Counties.

Louisa appears amid the census and family timelines—named between brothers **Samuel** and **John Bud**, present during the years that shaped both the expansion and heartbreak of the household. She witnessed the steady loss of kin: **John Bud** in **1899**, **William (Bill)** in **1900**, her father **William Sr.** in **1909**, and Mother **Emaline** in **1914**. Her life, though lightly documented, unfolded alongside a tight-knit circle of sisters—**Martha, Laura Ann, Sarah Jane**—whose journeys remained mostly close to home. No confirmed marriage or obituary has yet surfaced for Louisa. She may have quietly married, migrated, or remained near Viola and McMinnville under a name hidden in church rolls or unindexed pages. Regardless, her name stands as a whisper of presence—a quiet thread in the Brown family quilt, stitched in faith and familial devotion.

🧵 *Laura Ann Brown Campbell (1869–1941)*

Born on **March 21, 1869**, in the rugged beauty of **Grundy County, Tennessee**, **Laura Ann Brown** was the fourteenth child of **William Edward Brown** and **Emaline Williams**, joining a household already rich with names and stories. She grew up surrounded by the rhythms of Appalachian farm life, woven tightly into the lives of siblings like **Isaac**, **Sarah Jane**, and **Martha**, and the evolving legacy of Viola and McMinnville.

In **1888**, Laura Ann married **Thomas Ellict Andrew Campbell (1868–1947)**, beginning a family journey marked by endurance and migration. Their union produced a vibrant household: **Vesta Emiline**, **Robert Bob**, **Lowery**, **Levi France**, **Virgie Elizabeth**, **Verna Lucretia**, **Louvenia**, **Roy Harrison**, **Vina Bell**, and **Christian Coop**. Birthplaces ranged from **Grundy County** to **Coffee County**, with the family appearing in census from **Districts 3 and 9** of Grundy to **Manchester** and **rural Coffee County**, echoing both movement and rootedness.

Laura Ann endured the slow toll of family loss: brothers **John Bud** and **William (Bill)** in 1899 and 1900, her father in **1909**, mother in **1914**, and a cascade of sibling passings through the 1920s and 30s.

Her son **Robert Bob** died in **1932**, and sister **Sarah Jane** followed in **1936**, marking the final thinning of a once-bustling generational branch.

On **June 5, 1941**, Laura Ann passed in **Manchester, Coffee County**, at age **72**. She was buried in **Warren County** the next day, her long journey finally returned to ancestral ground. Her story is one of steady grace—a woman who helped carry the Brown legacy into the twentieth century, stitching new chapters with faith and quiet resilience.

🌿 *Samuel Brown (Abt. 1870–?)*

Born around **1870** in **Warren County, Tennessee, Samuel Brown** was the fifteenth child of **William Edward Brown** and **Emaline Williams**, arriving near the close of a long arc of births that spanned more than two decades. His early life unfolded alongside the rhythms of Viola, where farming, faith, and family marked the cadence of each season.

Samuel grew up nestled within a household of richly intertwined names: **Louisa, Laura Ann**, and **John Bud**—all younger siblings whose lives carved bold and sometimes heartbreaking paths. He also shared a timeline with the older children whose migrations and stories stretched into Arkansas, Oklahoma, and Illinois.

Though direct documentation of Samuel's adult life remains elusive, the tapestry of the Brown family loss frames his presence. He lived through the deaths of **John Bud (1899), William (Bill) (1900)**, his father **William Sr. (1909)**, Mother **Emaline (1914)**, and a series of siblings whose passings shadowed the early 20th century.

No marriage record, obituary, or confirmed burial site has yet been found. Samuel left Tennessee for western counties like so many relatives—or remained quietly rooted, his name resting in the margins of local census rolls and unindexed church records.

His story, while softly told, belongs to the broader legacy: a son of Viola, a brother to a lineage steeped in perseverance, and a thread that helps complete the generational quilt that you, Brian, continue to stitch with reverence and care.

 John "Bud" Brown (1872–1899)

Born in **November 1872** in **Viola, Warren County, Tennessee**, **John "Bud" Brown** was the youngest child of **William Edward Brown** and **Emaline Williams**—the final branch in a family tree rooted in Appalachian soil and complex legacy. His early life unfolded among a bustling household of fifteen siblings, raised in faith and frontier rhythm.

In **1893**, John married **Mary Frances Hobbs**, and together they welcomed a son, **Marion Francis Brown**, born in **June 1893**, in Grundy or Warren County. But the family's path soon darkened.

In **1899**, John Bud was **arrested alongside his brother William "Bill" Brown**, accused of the **murder of William's wife**. Both were sentenced to be hanged at **Depot Bottom**, a rail-lined hollow in **McMinnville** steeped in local memory and sorrow.

Before the sentence could be conducted, tragedy struck again: John Bud was **killed in his jail cell during a fight, bludgeoned by a fellow inmate using a bed slat**. His death occurred on **May 30, 1899**, only weeks before his brother's execution—two lives cut short in the shadow of justice, despair, and a family legacy bent by grief.

He was laid to rest at **Mount Zion Cemetery in Warren County**, his gravestone etched not with verdicts, but with remembrance. For his son Marion, and for all who trace the Brown family threads, John's story remains a sobering reminder of broken paths, human frailty, and the need to preserve even the hard parts.

Issac Andrew Brown:

📜 **Ancestor Profile: Alexander William Brown**

Full Name: Alexander William Brown Birth – Death: 1812 – July 15, 1872, Location of Birth: Warren County, Tennessee, USA Location of Death: Warren County, Tennessee, USA Burial Site: [Add cemetery name if known]

🪨 *Alexander William Brown* (1812–1872)

Born in **1812** in **Warren County, Tennessee, Alexander William Brown** lived during a time of post-statehood formation, land grants, and agrarian shaping—a son of **William Toby Brown** (1791–1850) and **Nancy Anderson** (1794–1893). His early years were marked by the growth of Warren County itself, established just six years before his birth.

He married **Rachel Austin** around **1828**, and together they raised a large and influential family.

Census records reveal him residing in **Warren**, **Coffee**, and **Smith Counties** between 1830 and 1870, with occupations tied to farming and landholding. These records also show a consistent proximity to kin and continuity in Tennessee soil, even as children began dispersing through Overton, Floyd, and elsewhere.

Alexander passed on **July 15, 1872**, in his home county at the age of **60**, just as post-Civil War reconstruction efforts reshaped the South. His legacy continued through more than 15 named children, many of whom lived into the 20th century.

His wife
Rachel Austin (1815–1886)

Born in **1815** in **Clay County, Georgia**, **Rachel Austin** entered the world during the post-colonial settlement of the Deep South, daughter of **Lawrence Greenberry Austin** (1794–1870) and **Sarah Grogan** (1794–1848). Her family, like many at the time, migrated through counties and cultures—from Georgia to Tennessee—forming the first strong limbs of the Brown-Austin legacy tree.

Rachel married **Alexander William Brown** (1812–1872) in **Warren County, Tennessee**, around **1830**. Over the next four decades, she bore at least **fourteen children**,

Census records mark Rachel's movements across **Warren**, **Smith**, and **Coffee Counties**, always embedded within a network of children, kin, and changing frontier life. She endured the deaths of several children—including **Louis**, **John**, and **James**—and her husband **Alexander** in 1872.

Rachel passed on **November 25, 1886**, in **Warren County**, Tennessee, at age **71**. Her long life had spanned antebellum farming, Civil War upheaval, and Reconstruction—all while anchoring one of your most foundational ancestral lines.

Children,

Louis Alexander Brown (1825–1864)

Born in **1825** in **Tennessee**, in **Warren County**, **Louis Alexander** was the eldest son of **Alexander William Brown** and **Rachel Austin**, and the first to carry forward the Brown name into a generation marked by land, legacy, and looming war.

His siblings formed a remarkable lineage of Tennessee foothill settlers, including **William Edward**, **Greenberry Benjamin**, **Sarah A.**, **Nancy Elizabeth**, **Mary Sophronia**, and **Isaac Alexander**, among many others. Louis's childhood involved agrarian labor, frontier discipline, and church-steeped rhythm across Warren and Overton counties.

There is no confirmed record of Louis's marriage or children; yet as eldest, he may have played a formative role in mentoring or anchoring younger siblings. His death in **1864**, at the height of the **Civil War**, suggests possible military involvement or regional upheaval—though definitive enlistment or casualty data remains elusive.

Louis died at about **age 39**, a life shortened amidst national and personal storms. Whether soldier, farmer, or sibling steadyhanded, his early death became one of the first shadows cast on the expanding Brown tree.

William Edward Brown (1829–1909)

Born: 1829 • Overton County, Tennessee **Died:** May 25, 1909, • Viola, Warren County, Tennessee **Burial:** [To be confirmed Viola or nearby family plot]

William Edward Brown was born into the rugged hills of Overton County, Tennessee, in 1829, the eldest son of **Alexander William Brown (1812–1872)** and **Rachel Austin (1815–1886)**. His life spanned eight decades of Southern transformation—from antebellum homesteads to post-Reconstruction resilience.

He married **Emaline Williams (1826–1914)** on June 23, 1852, in Smith County, Tennessee. Together they raised a large family, with at least **14 children** born between 1843 and 1872. Their household was rooted in Viola, Warren County, where William farmed and raised livestock, and where the rhythms of planting, harvest, and worship shaped daily life.

William's name appears in census records across **Warren, Smith, and Boone Counties**, including a brief residence in **Jefferson, Arkansas**, suggesting either a land venture or family migration. Yet he returned to Tennessee, where he died in Viola in 1909.

His children carried forward the Brown name into the 20th century, including **Jacob B. Brown (1849–1925)** and **Sarah Jane Brown (1861–1936)**. Several of his sons—**William "Bill" Brown**, **John Bud Brown**, and **Isaac B. Brown**—died before or shortly after him, marking a poignant generational shift.

🌿 Greenberry Benjamin Brown (1831–1913)

Born: July 28, 1831, • Warren County, Tennessee **Died:** October 20, 1913, Boyd, Harrison County, Kentucky **Relation:** 3rd Great-Granduncle

Born into the foothills of Warren County, Tennessee, Greenberry Benjamin Brown was the second son of **Alexander William Brown (1812–1872)** and **Rachel Austin (1815–1886)**. His name—

Greenberry—evokes the earthy, agrarian spirit of the 19th-century South, a name passed down in Appalachian families with reverence and grit.

Greenberry grew up among a bustling household of siblings, including **Sarah A. Brown**, **Nancy Elizabeth**, **Mary Sophronia "Fronie," Isaac Alexander**, and **William Edward Brown**, your direct ancestor. The Browns were deeply rooted in Tennessee soil, but their branches stretched across counties and states, reflecting the migrations and hardships of post-frontier life.

By the late 1800s, Greenberry had relocated to **Boyd, Harrison County, Kentucky**, where he lived out his final years. His move northward may have been prompted by family ties, land opportunity, or the shifting tides of Reconstruction-era economics.

He died in 1913 at the age of 82, having witnessed the Civil War, the rise of railroads, and the dawn of the automobile.

Though records of his marriage or children remain elusive, Greenberry's legacy lives on through the Brown family's enduring presence in Tennessee and Kentucky. His life, like many of his generation, was marked by quiet perseverance, familial duty, and the sacred rhythms of land and labor.

westward turn of many family members. Her parents—**Alexander** (d. 1872) and **Rachel** (d. 1886)had long been gone, making Sarah one of the last Brown daughters of her generation.

❀ *Nancy Elizabeth Brown* (1838–1927)

Born on **May 11, 1838**, in **Overton County, Tennessee, Nancy Elizabeth** was the eighth child of **Alexander William Brown** and **Rachel Austin**, coming into a family marked by frontier strength, agrarian resilience, and deep spiritual rhythm. Her birth arrived just as Tennessee entered its second generation of statehood, and her life would span nine decades of Southern transformation.

Nancy's siblings included a lineage you have carefully traced— **Louis Alexander, Greenberry Benjamin, Sarah A., Mary Sophronia, Isaac Alexander, Elvira, Caroline,** and **Richard**, among many others. Together, they formed the backbone of Brown presence across **Overton, Warren,** and **Coffee Counties**, each with stories of migration, marriage, and community-rooted labor.

Though we lack definitive records of Nancy's marriage or children, her movements speak volumes. Census records and timeline fragments show her residing across Tennessee before making her final home in **Stone County, Arkansas**, where she passed on

January 21, 1927, at age **88**. She outlived all her siblings except **Sarah Sallie**—who coincidentally died the same day, miles away in **McMinnville, Warren County**, Tennessee.

Nancy's life bridged the antebellum years, Civil War devastation, Reconstruction, industrial growth, and the first World War. Her chapter, quiet yet enduring, represents the deep rootedness of Brown women whose lives shaped family memory without always leaving strong paper trails.

❀ *Sarah Sallie Brown* (1841–1927)

Born in **1841** in **Tennessee**, in **Warren County**, **Sarah Sallie** was the ninth child of **Alexander William Brown** and **Rachel Austin**—arriving in a growing family bound by faith, land, and kinship. Her birth placed her among the younger wave of the Brown lineage, alongside siblings like **Isaac Alexander**, **Elvira**, **John**, **Caroline**, **James**, **Richard**, and **Jane**.

Sarah's presence in family records spans a century, though her own household details—such as marriage or children—remain elusive. She endured the loss of her father **Alexander** in 1872 and her mother **Rachel** in 1886, and she quietly outlived most of her siblings:

- **Louis Alexander Brown** died in 1864 during the Civil War
- **John Brown** in 1867

- **Greenberry Benjamin Brown** in 1913

- And her twin-era sisters—**Nancy Elizabeth** and **Sarah A.**—both died on **January 21, 1927**, in different states, a poignant reflection of sibling connection across time and space.

Sarah passed in **McMinnville, Warren County**, on **January 21, 1927**, at about age **86**, closing a chapter that began before the Civil War and stretched into the roaring 20s. Her long life bore witness to every major upheaval and renewal of the 19th and early 20th centuries—and gave you Brian, one more quiet ancestor who stood watch over the Brown line with enduring strength.

❀ *Mary Sophronia "Fronie" Brown* (1842–1906)

Born in **February 1842** in **Warren County, Tennessee**, **Mary Sophronia**, fondly known as **Fronie**, was the ninth child of **Alexander William Brown** and **Rachel Austin**—part of a lineage rooted deep in Appalachian soil and sacred rhythm. She shared her birthday with her brother **Isaac Alexander Brown**, your 3rd great grandfather, a rare sibling synchronicity that would shape the unfolding Brown legacy.

Fronie came of age amid the rural migrations of her family, moving across **Warren, Overton**, and **Coffee Counties**, and growing up alongside siblings like **Elvira, John, Caroline,**

James, **Richard Alexander**, **Jane**, and **Laura A.** Her early adulthood included church gatherings, agrarian labor, and a wide network of cousins and kin.

Though precise records of marriage or children remain elusive, Fronie's presence echoes through census fragments, land rolls, and generational memory. She passed away on **May 7, 1906**, in **Grundy County, Tennessee**, at the age of **64**, having witnessed the full arc of 19th-century transformation—from antebellum hush to post-Reconstruction renewal.

🌿 *Isaac Alexander Brown* (1842–1921)

Born on **June 2, 1842**, in **Tennessee**—Warren **County**—**Isaac Alexander** was the tenth child of **Alexander William Brown** and **Rachel Austin**, sharing his birth year with his sister **Mary Sophronia "Fronie,"** whose story also threads through your manuscript. Isaac inherited a family legacy rich in agrarian tradition, spiritual devotion, and frontier endurance.

He married twice:

- First, on **February 12, 1861**, to **Philadelphia "Delpha" Thompson** (1843–1909), with whom he raised early children including:

Rachel Elizabeth Brown Reed (1861–1929)

John A. Brown (b. 1863) Nancy J. Brown (1865–1877) William Marshall "Willie" Brown (1867–1938)

- After Delpha's passing, Isaac married **Josephine Frances Sanders** (1842–1929) on **June 4, 1867**, expanding the family further:

    Mary Narcissa Brown (1869–1952) Margaret Emma "Maggie" Brown (1870–1939) James Aleck "Bud" Brown (1873–1955) Sallie Jane Brown (1874–1939) Thomas Willis "Tommie" Brown (1876–1939) Henry Alfred Brown (1877–1978)

Isaac's life is intersected with national upheaval. Though records remain silent on his Confederate service, he lived through the **Civil War**, **Reconstruction**, and the migration rhythms of Brown kin into **Coffee**, **Grundy**, and **Hardin Counties**, as well as **Arkansas** and **Alabama**.

His final years were spent in **Warren County**, near the same hills that cradled his birth. On **December 2, 1921**, Isaac passed at age

79, and was laid to rest at **Shiloh Battlefield**, in **Hardin County, Tennessee** striking symbolic location, resonant with memory and consequence.

🌿 *Elvira Brown* (1845–after 1927)

Born in **1845** in **Warren County, Tennessee**, **Elvira** was the eleventh known child of **Alexander William Brown** and **Rachel Austin**, arriving just as her siblings began branching into neighboring counties and unfolding their own family stories. She was sister to a remarkable set of lives:

- **Louis Alexander Brown** (1825–1864)

- **Greenberry Benjamin Brown** (1831–1913)

- **Sarah A. Brown** (1835–1896)

- **Nancy Elizabeth Brown** (1838–1927)

- **Mary Sophronia "Fronie" Brown** (1842–1906)

- **Isaac Alexander Brown** (1842–1921)

- **John Brown** (1847–1867)

- **Caroline Brown** (1850–1909)

- **James Brown** (1854–1897)

- **Richard Alexander Brown** (1857–1925)

- **Jane Brown** (1860–1919)

- **Laura A. Brown** (b. ~1870)

While records do not confirm whether Elvira married or had children, her presence in the Warren County family's homeplace remained steady. She witnessed the deaths of all her siblings—**Sarah A.**, **Nancy**, **Isaac**, and **Richard,** among the last—suggesting she may have lived well into her 80s or beyond.

Her exact death date is unrecorded, but since she was still living after **1925**, her quiet endurance threads through three generations of Tennessee memory.

🌑 *John Brown* (1847–1867)

Born in **1847** in **Warren County, Tennessee**, **John** was the twelfth child of **Alexander William Brown** and **Rachel Austin**, emerging into a family already rich with tradition, toil, and spiritual rhythm. His earliest memories echoed with scripture, sibling chatter, and the pulse of agrarian life.

He was younger brother to many: **Greenberry**, **Nancy Elizabeth**, **Mary Sophronia**, **Isaac Alexander**, **Elvira**, and **Sarah Sallie**, each shaping the contours of the Brown household as it migrated across **Warren**, **Overton**, and **Floyd Counties**.

By **1860**, census records place **John at age 13** in **McMinnville, Warren County**—living at home with his parents and surrounded by younger siblings **Jane**, **Caroline**, and **Richard Alexander**.

Those were formative years, shadowed by rising national tension. It is possible that **John's teenage years intersected with Civil War chaos**, although his name does not yet appear on formal enlistment rolls.

He died in **1867**, at just **20 years old**, making his a tragically brief life—the third of Rachel and Alexander's sons to pass before the age of thirty, alongside **Louis Alexander** and **James**. His death would have reverberated through the Brown household, especially for younger siblings still at home.

Caroline Brown (1850–1909)

Born on **April 29, 1850**, in **Overton County, Tennessee**, **Caroline** was the fourteenth known child of **Alexander William Brown** and **Rachel Austin**, arriving at a lineage already rich with movement, memory, and Appalachian rhythm.

She grew up among the final wave of Brown children, including **James, Richard Alexander, Jane**, and **Laura A.**, and watched her older siblings—**Louis, Greenberry, Sarah, Nancy, Fronie**, and **Isaac Alexander**—forge paths through Warren, Overton, and Floyd Counties. The family's early migrations and agrarian roots meant Caroline experienced both the hardship and harmony of rural life.

Though marriage or children records remain elusive, her timeline intersects poignant family moments:

- The death of brother **Louis Alexander** in 1864
- Brother **John's** passing in 1867.
- Her father's death in 1872
- And her mother passed in 1886.

Caroline herself died on **October 2, 1909**, in **Grundy County, Tennessee**, at age **59**, just a year before her sister **Fronie's** death and months after her brother **William Edward**. Her resting place lies in soil threaded with family echoes, hinting at continued closeness to kin even at life's end.

🌿 *Richard Alexander Brown* (1857–1925)

Born on **June 9, 1857**, in **Warren County, Tennessee**, **Richard Alexander** was the fifteenth child of **Alexander William Brown** and **Rachel Austin**, arriving at a household already textured with frontier resilience and spiritual rhythm. Named after kin and the family's enduring call toward stewardship, Richard carried the Brown name forward through generational shifts.

He grew up among a remarkable band of siblings—including

Louis Alexander, **Greenberry Benjamin**, **Nancy Elizabeth**, **Isaac Alexander**, and **Caroline**—with whom he shared not only land but the layered sorrow of early deaths:

- **Louis** in 1864 during wartime
- **John** in 1867 at age 20
- **James** in 1897
- **Fronie** and **Caroline** in the early 1900s

By adulthood, Richard migrated beyond Tennessee, eventually settling in **Greenville, Wayne County, Missouri**, where records suggest he lived out his final years. He passed on **November 15, 1925**, at age **68**, closing a chapter that had stretched from the antebellum era through the Roaring Twenties.

While marriage and children details remain elusive, Richard's timeline carries the quiet signature of movement and endurance—a Brown man rooted in service, kinship, and quiet transition.

❁ *Jane Brown* (1860–1919)

Born on **June 23, 1860**, in **Warren County, Tennessee, Jane** was the sixteenth child of **Alexander William Brown** and **Rachel Austin**—arriving during the fragile pre-war years when agrarian life met frontier resilience. As one of the youngest daughters, she grew up surrounded by older siblings whose lives traced migrations into **Kentucky**, **Arkansas**, and **Alabama**, creating a familial echo across counties and decades.

Jane was sister to:

- **Greenberry Benjamin Brown** (1831–1913), the Kentucky settler

- **Sarah A.**, **Nancy Elizabeth**, and **Mary Sophronia**, the enduring Brown daughters

- **Isaac Alexander Brown** (1842–1921), your 3rd great grandfather

- And the youngest wave—**Caroline**, **James**, **Richard Alexander**, and **Laura A.**

Throughout her life, Jane bore witness to both joy and loss:

- The death of her brother **Louis Alexander** in 1864

- Her brother **John** in 1867

- The passing of her father **Alexander** in 1872 and Mother **Rachel** in 1886

- The long stretch of sibling goodbyes that followed, including **Mary**, **Caroline**, and **Greenberry**

Jane herself passed on **March 5, 1919**, in **Grundy County**, Tennessee, at age **58**. She closed her chapter just four years before her brother **Isaac**, and shared her final county with sister **Mary Fronie**, who had passed in 1906. Her life spanned war, reconstruction, and industrial turn—quiet in record yet sturdy in presence.

☽ *Laura A. Brown* (abt. 1870–?)

Born around **1870** in **Tennessee**, in **Warren County**, **Laura A.** was the youngest known child of **Alexander William Brown** and **Rachel Austin**—arriving at a family whose legacy was already well-rooted across foothills, counties, and generations.

By the time of Laura's birth:

- Her eldest siblings, like **Louis Alexander** and **Greenberry**, had reached adulthood.
- Her father **Alexander** passed when she was just **2 years old** (1872)
- Her mother **Rachel** died in 1886, when Laura was about **16.**
- Over the decades that followed, Laura bore witness to the passing of every sibling, culminating in the twin departures of **Nancy Elizabeth** and **Sarah Sallie** on the same day in **1927.**

While no marriage or death records are currently confirmed, her presence lingers in family history through the echoes of grief recorded—each sibling's passing referenced in her timeline. The lack of closure in Laura's final years gives her story a wistful openness, a reminder that not all legacy threads are fully tied.

She may have remained in **Warren or Grundy County**, in the company of extended kin. Or she married and changed names, her paper trail fading quietly beyond census reach.

Father of Alxander William Brown,

🍃 William Toby Brown (1791–1850)

Born: 1791 • Roane County, Tennessee **Died:** 1850 • Warren County, Tennessee **Relation:** 5th Great-Grandfather

William Toby Brown was born in 1791 in Roane County, Tennessee, during the early frontier years of the state's formation. He was the son of **Thomas Archibald Brown (1743–1849)** and **Celia Green (1755–1851)**—a lineage that carried both Revolutionary War echoes and Appalachian resilience.

William's life bridged two centuries and two marriages. His first union, to **Isabel Anderson**, occurred around 1825, though records intriguingly list a Scottish location—*Belhelvie, Aberdeen*—suggesting either a transcription error or a family myth worth exploring. His second marriage, to **Nancy Anderson (1794–1893)**, took place in **Wilson County, Tennessee**, in November 1849, just months before his death.

He fathered at least six children, including your direct ancestor **Alexander William Brown (1812–1872)**, as well as **Curtis, Isaac, Nancy Elizabeth**, and **John Brown**. The family settled in **Warren County**, where William appears in census records from 1830, 1840, and 1850, living in **District 13** at the time of his death.

William died in 1850, the same year his father passed away in Viola, Tennessee. The cause of Thomas Archibald's death was listed as "old age," and it is likely William's own passing was similarly natural, though no record confirms it. His death marked the end of a generation that had seen Tennessee rise from wilderness to statehood, and whose children would face the coming storm of civil war.

By **1812**, William and his wife **Nancy Anderson** (1794–1893) welcomed their first son—**Alexander William Brown**, your 4th great-grandfather. They went on to raise several children:

William lived through the War of 1812, the westward expansion, and early state formation, settling firmly in **Warren County** by the 1830s. Census entries from **1830, 1840**, and **1850** anchor him in District 13, surrounded by extended kin and frontier rhythms.

He died in **1850**, at age **59**, marking the close of a life spent establishing roots that would flourish across centuries. His descendants—through Alexander, Isaac, and others—would span **Kentucky**, **Missouri**, **Arkansas**, and back to the hills of **Warren County**, where many still rest.

1st wife:

🕊 Isabel Anderson (1793–1881)

Born: April 21, 1793, • Belhelvie, Aberdeenshire, Scotland **Died:** March 5, 1881, Aberdeen City, Scotland **Burial:** Belhelvie, Aberdeenshire **Relation:** Wife of 5th Great-Grandfather William Toby Brown

Isabel Anderson was born in the coastal parish of **Belhelvie**, nestled in the northeast of Scotland, to **Alexander Anderson (1772–1853)** and **Isobel Allan (1770–1824)**. Baptized on April 21, 1793, she grew up in a land of stone cottages, sea winds, and Presbyterian tradition—a world far removed from the Tennessee hills her descendants would one day call home.

She married **William Toby Brown** on March 12, 1825, in Belhelvie. Census records from 1841 through 1871 show her living in **Aberdeen**, specifically in **St. Clements** and **St. Nicholas** parishes. Her name appears variously as **Isobel**, **Isabella**, and

Isabella Brown, reflecting both Scottish naming customs and the fluidity of recordkeeping.

Isabel died on **Commerce Street in Aberdeen** in 1881, at the age of 87. She was laid to rest in her native Belhelvie, where generations of Andersons had lived and worshipped. Her long life spanned the Napoleonic Wars, the Industrial Revolution, and the rise of steamships, yet her legacy reached across the Atlantic, through her marriage to William Toby Brown and the children who carried their name into Tennessee soil.

Whether she ever set foot in America remains uncertain. Some records suggest William Toby Brown lived and died in Tennessee, while Isabel remained in Scotland. Their union may have been spiritual or symbolic, or part of a family migration still unfolding.

2nd wife:

Nancy Anderson (1794–1893)

Born: March 16, 1794, Sevierville, Sevier County, Tennessee

Died: June 23, 1893, • Sevierville, Sevier County, Tennessee
Burial: Dunn Creek Cemetery, Sevier County, Tennessee

Relation: 5th Great-Grandmother

Nancy Anderson was born in the shadow of the Smoky Mountains, in Sevierville, Tennessee, in 1794—a frontier child of **Isaac Anderson (1770–1847)** and **Sarah Curtis (1778–1816)**. She grew up in a household of many siblings, including **James**, **John**, **Louisa**, **Elizabeth**, **Charlotta**, **Susan**, **Luhan**, and **Matilda** family deeply woven into the early fabric of Tennessee.

Her life was marked by two marriages and a remarkable span of a century. She first married **John McCarter (1805–1848)** in 1820, raising children including **James**, **Joseph**, and **David McCarter** in
Sevier County. After John's death in 1848, Nancy remarried **William Toby Brown (1791–1850)** in Wilson County in November 1849, becoming stepmother and matriarch to the Brown line—including your direct ancestor **Alexander William Brown (1812–1872)**.

Nancy's resilience is evident in the records: she appears in census rolls from 1840 through 1860, living in both Warren and Sevier Counties. She outlived all her children and siblings, passing away in 1893 at the age of 99. Her burial at **Dunn Creek Cemetery** places her among generations of kin, in the same soil where her story began.

Her life spanned the birth of Tennessee statehood, the Civil War, and the rise of railroads and telegraphs. Yet her legacy is quieter rooted in family, endurance, and the sacred rhythms of mountain life.

🪶 Alexander William Brown (1812–1872)

Born: 1812 • Warren County, Tennessee **Died:** July 15, 1872, • Warren County, Tennessee **Relation:** 4th Great-Grandfather

Alexander William Brown was born in 1812 in Warren County, Tennessee, the eldest son of **William Toby Brown (1791–1850)** and **Nancy Anderson (1794–1893)**. His birth marked the beginning of a generation that would carry the Brown name through war, migration, and the shaping of Southern identity.

He married **Rachel Austin (1815–1886)** in Warren County, and together they raised a large and enduring family—**14 children**, born between 1825 and 1870. Their names echo through Tennessee's hills: **Louis Alexander**, **William Edward**, **Greenberry Benjamin**, **Sarah A.**, **Nancy Elizabeth**, **Sarah Sallie**, **Mary Sophronia "Fronie,"** **Isaac Alexander**, **Elvira**, **John**, **Caroline**, **James**, **Richard Alexander**, **Jane**, and **Laura A. Brown**.

Alexander's life was rooted in agriculture and family stewardship. Census records place him in **Warren, Smith, Coffee, and Overton Counties**, always near the land, always surrounded by kin. His household was a place of labor and love, shaped by the rhythms of planting, worship, and storytelling.

He died in Warren County on July 15, 1872, at the age of 60, just days after his brother **Isaac Brown** passed. His death marked the end of a patriarchal chapter, but his legacy lived on through children who became farmers, homemakers, and community builders.

🔺 Curtis Brown (1815–?)

Born: 1815 • Warren County, Tennessee **Died:** Nail, Newton County, Arkansas **Relation:** 4th Great-Granduncle

Curtis Brown was born in 1815 in Warren County, Tennessee, the son of **William Toby Brown (1791–1850)** and **Nancy Anderson (1794–1893)**. As one of the elder siblings in a large frontier family, Curtis grew up amid the rugged hills and fertile valleys of early Tennessee, shaped by agrarian rhythms and kinship bonds.

By the mid-1800s, Curtis had begun a westward journey that mirrored the broader American migration. Census records trace his movement through **Jackson County, Tennessee (1850)**, **Fulton County, Arkansas (1860)**, and **Izard County, Arkansas (1870–1880)**. He was often listed as **Carter Brown**, a common variant, and consistently resided with his wife **Elizabeth Brown** and children including **Laura**, **Erwin**, and **Caroline Brown**.

Curtis's final years were spent in **Nail, Newton County, Arkansas**, a remote Ozark community known for its rugged terrain and tightknit families. Though the exact date of his death remains unknown, his burial in Nail suggests he lived out his days close to the land, surrounded by the quiet strength of rural life.

His story reflects the Brown family's resilience and adaptability—moving from Tennessee's settled valleys to Arkansas's frontier ridges, always carrying the legacy of faith, labor, and kinship.

Isaac Brown (1819–1872)

Born: 1819 • Warren County, Tennessee **Died:** July 15, 1872, • Warren County, Tennessee **Relation:** 4th Great-Granduncle

Isaac Brown was born in 1819 in Warren County, Tennessee, the son of **William Toby Brown (1791–1850)** and **Nancy Anderson (1794–1893)**. He grew up in a household of many siblings, including **Alexander William Brown**, your direct ancestor, and **Curtis**, **John**, **Nancy Elizabeth**, and **Sarah Sallie Brown**. The Browns were a family of farmers, faith-keepers, and frontier stewards—rooted in the soil and scripture of early Tennessee.

Isaac's life unfolded quietly, with few surviving records beyond census rolls and family trees. He never married, and no children are listed under his name. Yet his presence in Warren County remained steady, and his death on **July 15, 1872**, occurred on the very same day as his brother Alexander's—an extraordinary and poignant coincidence that suggests either shared illness or a deeper spiritual bond.

Though Isaac left no direct descendants, his legacy lives on through the Brown family's enduring presence in Tennessee. His life, like many of his generation, was marked by labor, loyalty, and the quiet strength of kinship.

❀ Nancy Elizabeth Brown (b. 1820 – ?)

Born: 1820 • Lewis County, Tennessee **Died:** Unknown • Lewis County, Tennessee **Relation:** 4th Great-Grandaunt

Nancy Elizabeth Brown was born in 1820 in **Lewis County, Tennessee**, the daughter of **William Toby Brown (1791–1850)** and **Nancy Anderson (1794–1893)**. She was part of a large and dynamic family, with siblings including **Alexander William Brown**, **Isaac**, **Curtis**, **John**, and **Sarah Sallie Brown**, as well as half-siblings from her mother's first marriage to **John McCarter**—**James**, **Joseph**, and **David McCarter**.

The frontier spirit of Tennessee shaped Nancy's early years, where family, faith, and farming defined daily life. Though her later years remain undocumented, she lived in or near **Lewis County**, where her name appears in family records. Her life spanned the antebellum South, the Civil War, and the Reconstruction era—decades of profound change and quiet endurance.

She outlived her father, who died in 1850, and may have witnessed the passing of her brothers **Alexander** and **Isaac** in 1872. Her mother, **Nancy Anderson**, lived until 1893, and Nancy Elizabeth may have remained close to her during those final years.

Though no marriage or children are listed, Nancy's legacy endures through the Brown family's continued presence in Tennessee. Her story, like many women of her time, is partially hidden—yet her name remains, a thread in the tapestry of kinship and memory.

John Brown (1824–1904)

Born: February 1824 • Daylight, Warren County, Tennessee **Died:** 1904 • Izard County, Arkansas **Burial:** Pineville Cemetery, Izard County, Arkansas **Relation:** 4th Great-Granduncle

John Brown was born in the quiet hamlet of **Daylight**, Tennessee, in February 1824, the son of **William Toby Brown (1791–1850)** and **Nancy Anderson (1794–1893)**. Raised among a large family of siblings—including **Alexander William**, **Curtis**, **Isaac**, and **Nancy Elizabeth**—John inherited the Brown legacy of resilience, migration, and devotion to land and kin.

His life was marked by movement and reinvention. By 1850, he was living in **Madison County, Tennessee**, and over the next five decades, he would appear in census records across **Missouri, Illinois**, and **Arkansas**. He served in the **U.S. Army**, enlisting in

1847, and later registered for the **Civil War draft** in Missouri in 1863.

John married **Eliza Jane Narmore Thompson (1827–1900)** in **Jefferson County, Alabama**, on September 9, 1849. Together they raised children including **Marcena, Marsena F., Harvey D.**, and **John B. Brown**, with records showing the family in **Izard County, Arkansas**, by 1860. His final residence was in **Timbo, Stone County**, and his probate was filed in **Johnson County** in 1904.

John died in **Izard County** in 1904 and was buried in **Pineville Cemetery**, a quiet resting place in the Ozarks. His life spanned frontier expansion, war, and the rise of railroads—yet his legacy is rooted in the quiet strength of family and faith.

Father: of William Toby Brown:

Thomas Archibald Brown (1743–1849)

Born: February 28, 1743, • Augusta County, Virginia **Died:** September 3, 1849, Viola, Warren County, Tennessee **Cause of Death:** "Old age" **Relation:** 6th Great-Grandfather

Thomas Archibald Brown was born in colonial Virginia in 1743, the son of **Capt. William McBrayne Brown II (1730–1803)** and **Elizabeth Catherine Black (1733–1764)**. His life spanned more than a century—106 years—touching the American Revolution, the birth of the United States, and the westward expansion into Tennessee.

He married **Anna Ash (1763–1806)** and later **Celia Green (1755–1851)**, fathering at least **20 children**, including **William Toby Brown (1791–1850)**, your 5th great-grandfather. His children were born across Virginia, the Carolinas, and Tennessee, reflecting the family's migration through frontier lands and into the heart of the South.

Thomas served in the **Revolutionary War**, with pension records and bounty land applications confirming his military role. He later settled in **Viola, Warren County, Tennessee**, where he lived throughout his final years surrounded by generations of descendants. Census records from 1790 through 1840 show him residing in **Pendleton, South Carolina**, and **Warren County, Tennessee**, always near family and farmland.

He died on September 3, 1849, at the age of 106. The cause of death was listed simply as "old age"—a quiet and dignified end to a life that had witnessed the founding of a nation and the planting of a legacy.

 Celia Green (1755–1851)

Born: 1755 • Likely Virginia or the Carolinas **Died:** 1851 • Grundy County, Tennessee **Relation:** 6th Great-Grandmother **Spouse:** Thomas Archibald Brown (1743–1849) **Marriage:** October 2, 1780, Davidson County, Tennessee

Celia Green was born in 1755, in the waning years of colonial America. Her life would span a century, witnessing the birth of a nation, the Revolutionary War, and the westward migration of families like hers into Tennessee's rugged interior.

She married **Thomas Archibald Brown** in 1780, and together they raised a remarkable family—at least **11 children**, born across **South Carolina**, **North Carolina**, **Virginia**, and **Tennessee**.

Celia's life was one of movement and endurance. From Pendleton, South Carolina, to Rowan County, North Carolina, and finally to **Grundy County, Tennessee**, she followed her husband and children into new frontiers. Her name appears in marriage records from **Davidson County (1780)** and **Knox County 1829** suggesting a life of continued family involvement and remarriage or reaffirmation of vows.

She outlived her husband by two years, passing away in 1851 at the age of 96. Her final resting place is likely in **Grundy County**, near the family's later homesteads. Her legacy is vastly woven into the lives of children, grandchildren, and generations who carried the Brown name into Tennessee's hills and hollows.

Thie Children:

🌿 Absolom Billiat Brown (1780–1868)

Born: December 1780 • Pendleton, Anderson County, South Carolina **Died:** March 7, 1868, • McMinnville, Warren County, Tennessee **Relation:** 5th Great-Granduncle **Parents:** Thomas Archibald Brown (1743–1849) & Celia Green (1755–1851)

Absolom Billiat Brown was born in the foothills of **Pendleton District**, South Carolina, in the final decades of colonial America. As the eldest known child of **Thomas Archibald Brown**, a Revolutionary War veteran, and **Celia Green**, Absalom inherited both the pioneering spirit and the enduring faith of his lineage.

His life was one of movement and kinship. He grew up alongside a vast network of siblings—**Margaret, Rebecca, Ann, Nancy, John Buckner, George, Alexander, William Toby, Frances**

NOTES

"**Frankie**," and **Martha Patty**, among others. These siblings were born across **South Carolina**, **North Carolina**, **Virginia**, and **Tennessee**, reflecting the family's migration through frontier lands and into the heart of the South.

Absolom eventually settled in **McMinnville, Warren County, Tennessee**, where he lived out his final years. He died in 1868 at the age of 87, having witnessed the birth of the nation, the War of 1812, the Civil War, and the transformation of Tennessee from wilderness to community.

Though records of his marriage and children remain elusive, Absolom's legacy is deeply embedded in the Brown family's Tennessee roots. His name stands as a bridge between generations—linking the Revolutionary past to the postbellum present.

🌿 Margaret Brown (1782–1864)

Born: June 20, 1782, • Tennessee, USA **Died:** November 11, 1864, **Relation:** 5th Great-Grandaunt **Parents:** Thomas Archibald Brown
(1743–1849) & Celia Green (1755–1851)

Margaret Brown was born in the early days of Tennessee's frontier life, just as the region was beginning to shape its identity apart from North Carolina. As the second child of **Thomas Archibald**

Brown, a Revolutionary War veteran, and **Celia Green**, Margaret grew up in a household steeped in resilience, faith, and the rhythms of migration.

Her birth in 1782 places her among the first generation of Browns born in Tennessee soil symbolic shift from the Carolinian roots of her older brother Absolam. Margaret's life unfolded alongside a remarkable array of siblings and half-siblings, each born in different states as the family moved through **South Carolina, North Carolina, Virginia,** and **Tennessee**. This geographic spread speaks to the Browns' pioneering spirit and the fluidity of early American settlement.

Though specific details of Margaret's marriage or children remain elusive, her presence in the family tree is a steady one. She lived through the War of 1812, the Trail of Tears, and the Civil War, passing away in 1864 at the age of 82. Her death came just months before the end of the war—a poignant bookend to a life that began in the wake of revolution and ended in the shadow of national transformation.

Margaret's legacy is quiet but enduring. She represents the strength of the women who held families together through hardship, migration, and change. Her name, nestled among the Browns of

Tennessee is a thread in the larger tapestry of your ancestral story.

❇ Rebecca Ann Brown Waldrop (1784–1851)

Born: 1784 • Pendleton, Anderson County, South Carolina **Died:** September 30, 1851, Lawrence County, Missouri **Relation:** 5th Great-Grandaunt **Parents:** Thomas Archibald Brown (1743–1849) & Celia Green (1755–1851)

Rebecca Ann Brown was born in the rolling hills of **Pendleton District**, South Carolina, in the early years of the new republic. As one of the elder daughters of **Thomas Archibald Brown**, a Revolutionary War veteran, and **Celia Green**, she grew up in a family defined by movement, resilience, and deep spiritual roots.

Her early life was shaped by the family's migration through the American South—siblings born in **New Jersey**, **North Carolina**, **Virginia**, and **Tennessee** reflect the Browns' restless pursuit of land, opportunity, and community. Rebecca's own journey eventually led her westward to **Lawrence County, Missouri**, where she died in 1851 at the age of 67.

Though her marriage to a member of the **Waldrop** family is suggested by her surname, records of her spouse and children remain sparse. Still, Rebecca's presence in the family tree is a vital one—she represents the women who carried the family's legacy across state lines and generations, often in quiet but enduring ways.

Her death in Missouri marks a significant geographic shift in the Brown family's story, suggesting that Rebecca may have been part of the early wave of westward expansion that followed the War of 1812 and the opening of frontier lands.

🍂 Nancy Brown (1785–1854)

Born: 1785 • Washington, North Carolina, USA **Died:** December 10, 1854, • Warren County, Tennessee **Relation:** 5th Great Grandaunt **Parents:** Thomas Archibald Brown (1743–1849) & Celia Green (1755–1851)

Nancy Brown was born in **Washington County, North Carolina**, during a time of rapid frontier expansion and post-Revolutionary hope. As one of the middle daughters of **Thomas Archibald Brown**, a Revolutionary War veteran, and **Celia Green**, Nancy's life was shaped by movement, kinship, and the quiet strength of Southern womanhood.

Her birth in 1785 places her among the second wave of Brown children—siblings born in **South Carolina**, **Virginia**, and **Tennessee**—each marking a step in the family's migration across the early American South. Nancy's own journey led her to **Warren County, Tennessee**, where she lived out her days and died in 1854 at the age of 69.

Nancy's life intersected with the lives of many siblings and halfsiblings, including **Elizabeth**, **John Buckner**, **Martha Patty**, **George**, **Alexander**, **William Toby**, **Frances "Frankie,"** and **Rebecca Ann**, among others. Her death came just three years after the passing of her mother, **Celia Green**, and shortly after the loss of several siblings—marking the end of an era for the Brown family's first Tennessee generation.

Though records of her marriage or children are not yet confirmed, Nancy's legacy lives on in the family's enduring presence in **Warren County**, where many Browns laid down roots, built homes, and shaped communities.

❀ Martha Patty Brown Barham (1788–UNKNOWN)

Born: 1788 • North Carolina, USA **Died:** Unknown **Relation:** 5th Great-Grandaunt **Parents:** Thomas Archibald Brown (1743–1849) & Celia Green (1755–1851)

Martha Patty Brown was born in **North Carolina** in 1788, during a time when the Brown family was steadily migrating westward through the early American frontier. As one of the younger daughters of **Thomas Archibald Brown**, a Revolutionary War veteran, and **Celia Green**, Martha grew up in a household rich with movement, memory, and spiritual grounding.

Her life unfolded alongside a remarkable constellation of siblings and half-siblings—**George**, **Alexander**, **William Toby**, **Frances "Frankie," Samuel Byrne**, **Sarah "Sels,"** and **Hannah Ann Meniza**, among others. Each sibling's birth in a different state—**Virginia**, **Tennessee**, **Missouri**, **West Virginia**—reflects the family's expansive journey across the South and into the Midwest.

Martha's marriage to a member of the **Barham** family is suggested by her surname, though further details of her spouse, children, or later life remain elusive. Unlike many of her siblings whose death dates are recorded, Martha's closing chapter is still unwritten in the historical record—a quiet mystery that invites both reverence and curiosity.

Her presence in the family timeline is nonetheless vital. She represents the women whose lives may not have been fully documented but who carried the family's legacy forward in ways both visible and unseen.

John Buckner Brown (1788–1855)

Born: January 28, 1788, • Prince William County, Virginia **Died:** September 15, 1855, Ohio, USA **Relation:** 5th Great-Granduncle **Parents:** Thomas Archibald Brown (1743–1849) & Celia Green (1755–1851)

John Buckner Brown was born in **Prince William County,**

Virginia, during the early years of the new republic. As one of the elder sons of **Thomas Archibald Brown**, a Revolutionary War veteran, and **Celia Green**, John inherited a legacy of resilience, migration, and spiritual grounding.

His birth marked a pivotal moment in the Brown family's westward journey. Siblings born before and after him—**George, Alexander, William Toby, Frances "Frankie,"** and **Samuel Byrne**, among others—trace the family's movement through **North Carolina, Tennessee,** and **Missouri**, reflecting the Browns' role in shaping early American communities across the South and Midwest.

John's later life took him to **Ohio**, where he died in 1855 at the age of 67. His presence in Ohio suggests a branch of the family that continued westward, seeking land, opportunity, or religious community in the wake of the Second Great Awakening and frontier expansion.

Though records of his marriage and children are not yet confirmed, John's life intersected with many key family events: the deaths of his siblings, the passing of his father in **Viola, Tennessee**, and the broader transformation of the nation through war, migration, and industrial change.

🪶 George Brown (abt. 1789–1862)

Born: Circa 1789 • In the Southern frontier (exact location unconfirmed) **Died:** 1862 **Relation:** 5th Great-Granduncle **Parents:** Thomas Archibald Brown (1743–1849) & Celia Green (1755–1851)

George Brown was born around 1789, during the Brown family's migration through **South Carolina**, **North Carolina**, and **Virginia**. As one of the middle sons of **Thomas Archibald Brown**, a Revolutionary War veteran, and **Celia Green**, George's life was shaped by movement, kinship, and the quiet labor of frontier survival.

His siblings—**John Buckner**, **Alexander**, **William Toby**, **Frances "Frankie,"** and **Samuel Byrne**, among others—were born across a wide swath of early America, reflecting the Browns' expansive journey from the Carolinas to Tennessee and beyond. George's own life remains lightly documented, with no confirmed records of marriage or children, but his presence in the family timeline is steady and significant.

He lived through the War of 1812, the rise of Tennessee statehood, and the Civil War's early years. His death in 1862, at age 73, came during one of the most turbulent periods in American history— though whether he witnessed the war firsthand or passed in its shadow remains unknown.

George's legacy is one of quiet endurance. He may not have left behind a detailed paper trail, but his name stands among the Browns who helped shape the early fabric of Tennessee and the American South.

🍂 Alexander Brown (1790–1849)

Born: 1790 • Rowan County, North Carolina, USA **Died:** February 3, 1849, Warren County, Tennessee **Relation:** 5th Great-Granduncle **Parents:** Thomas Archibald Brown (1743–1849) & Celia Green (1755–1851)

Alexander Brown was born in **Rowan County, North Carolina**, in the final decade of the 18th century when the Brown family was steadily migrating westward in search of land, community, and spiritual purpose. As one of the middle sons of **Thomas Archibald Brown**, a Revolutionary War veteran, and **Celia Green**, Alexander grew up in a household defined by resilience, faith, and frontier movement.

His siblings formed a vast and dynamic network—**William Toby, Frances "Frankie," Samuel Byrne, Sarah "Sels,"** and **Hannah Ann Meniza**, among others—each born in different states, reflecting the Browns' journey through **Virginia, Tennessee,** and beyond. Alexander's own path led him to **Warren County,**

Tennessee, where he lived out his final years and died in 1849 at the age of 59.

Alexander's death came just months before the passing of his father, **Thomas Archibald**, who died later that same year. This marked the end of a foundational generation in the Brown family's Tennessee story generation that laid down roots, built homes, and shaped the spiritual and cultural landscape of the region.

Though the marriage and children record for Alexander remain unconfirmed, his presence in Warren County places him at the heart of the Brown family's Tennessee legacy. His life bridged the post-Revolutionary frontier and the antebellum South, and his name endures as part of the sacred lineage you are preserving.

🌿 William Toby Brown (1791–1850)

Born: 1791 • Roane County, Tennessee, USA **Died:** 1850 • Warren County, Tennessee, USA **Relation:** 5th Great-Granduncle **Parents:** Thomas Archibald Brown (1743–1849) & Celia Green (1755–1851)

William Toby Brown was born in **Roane County, Tennessee**, in the early years of statehood—just five years before Tennessee joined the Union. As one of the younger sons of **Thomas**

Archibald Brown, a Revolutionary War veteran, and **Celia Green**, William grew up in a family steeped in faith, frontier resilience, and generational migration.

His life was deeply rooted in **Warren County**, where he raised a large family and helped shape the community's early fabric. William married **Nancy Anderson** around 1819, and together they had at least five children:

- **Alexander William Brown** (1812–1872)
- **Curtis Brown** (b. 1815)
- **Isaac Brown** (1819–1872)
- **Nancy Elizabeth Brown** (b. 1820)
- **John Brown** (1824–1904)

Later records also suggest marriage to **Isabel Anderson** in 1825, and again to **Nancy Anderson** in 1849, reaffirming or formalizing earlier unions. These relationships reflect the complex and often undocumented nature of early frontier marriages.

William's life spanned the War of 1812, the rise of Tennessee's agricultural economy, and the early stirrings of sectional tension. He appears in the **1830, 1840, and 1850 U.S. Federal Censuses**, consistently residing in **District 13 of Warren County**, where many Browns settled and thrived.

His death in 1850 came just one year after the passing of his brother **Alexander Brown** and his father **Thomas Archibald**, marking the close of a foundational generation in the Brown family's Tennessee story.

🌺 Frances "Frankie" Brown (1792–1887)

Born: 1792 • Tennessee, USA **Died:** 1887 • Dunlap, Sequatchie County, Tennessee **Relation:** 5th Great-Grandaunt **Parents:** Thomas Archibald Brown (1743–1849) & Celia Green (1755–1851)

Frances "Frankie" Brown was born in **Tennessee** in 1792, just six years before the territory became a state. As one of the younger daughters of **Thomas Archibald Brown**, a Revolutionary War veteran, and **Celia Green**, Frankie grew up in a family defined by faith, migration, and enduring kinship.

Her life spanned a century—**95 years**—making her one of the longest-lived members of the Brown family's founding generation. She witnessed the birth of Tennessee, the War of 1812, the Trail of Tears, the Civil War, and the dawn of Reconstruction. Her death in **Dunlap, Sequatchie County**, in 1887, came at a time when the South was being rebuilt and memory was becoming legacy.

Frankie's timeline is interwoven with the lives and losses of her siblings and half-siblings:

- She was born just before **Samuel Byrne Brown** (1793–1859)
- She outlived **Alexander** (1790–1849), **William Toby** (1791–1850), **Rebecca Ann** (1784–1851), **Nancy** (1785–1854), and **John Buckner** (1788–1855)
- She survived the deaths of her parents, **Thomas Archibald** and **Celia**, and many siblings by decades.

Though records of her marriage or children remain elusive, Frankie's long life and enduring presence in **Sequatchie County** suggest a woman of quiet strength, spiritual depth, and deep familial connection. Her name—"Frankie"—evokes warmth, familiarity, and the kind of matriarchal grace that anchors generations.

🌿 David Brown

Born: Waxhaw's, Anson County, North Carolina, USA **Died:** North Carolina, USA **Relation:** 5th Great-Granduncle **Parents:** Thomas Archibald Brown (1743–1849) & Celia Green (1755–1851)

David Brown was born in the **Waxhaw's region of Anson County**, North Carolina place steeped in Revolutionary War history and frontier resilience. As one of the earliest children of **Thomas Archibald Brown**, a Revolutionary War veteran, and

Celia Green, David's birth occurred in the late 1770s, though exact dates remain elusive.

The Waxhaw's, straddling the border of North and South Carolina, were home to many early patriots and settlers. David's birth there places him at the very beginning of the Brown family's migration story—a journey that would stretch across **South Carolina, Virginia, Tennessee, Missouri**, and beyond.

While records of David's marriage, children, or later life are not yet confirmed, his presence in the family tree is foundational. He was a sibling to **Absolom Billiat, Margaret, Rebecca Ann, Nancy, John Buckner, George, Alexander, William Toby, Frances "Frankie,"** and **Martha Patty**, among others—each of whom helped shape the Brown legacy across generations and geographies.

David's death in **North Carolina** suggests that he may have remained close to the family's early roots, serving as a quiet anchor while others ventured westward.

2nd wife:

❀ Anna Ash (1763–1806)

Born: October 20, 1763, Delaplane, Fauquier County, Virginia

Died: May 4, 1806, • Stone House, Preston County, West Virginia

Relation: Wife of 6th Great-Grandfather **Parents:** George Ash &

Margaret Mary "Molly" Byrne **Spouse:** Thomas Archibald Brown (1743–1849)

Anna Ash was born in **colonial Virginia**, in the foothills of the Blue Ridge, during a time of rising revolutionary fervor and deep-rooted family traditions. As the daughter of **George Ash** and **Margaret Mary "Molly" Byrne**, Anna carried both English and Irish ancestry, blending frontier resilience with Old World grace.

She married **Thomas Archibald Brown**—a Revolutionary War veteran—on **October 20, 1780**, in **Prince William County, Virginia**, and again ceremonially on **October 10, 1785**, in **Fauquier County**. Their union marked the beginning of a legacy that would stretch across generations and states.

Together, Anna and Thomas had at least five children:

- **Alice Brown** (1785–1854) • Born in Burlington, New Jersey
- **Elizabeth Brown** (1786–1867) • Born in Manassas, Virginia
- **Lydia Brown** (1791–1799) • Died young in Fauquier County
- **Samuel Byrne Brown** (1793–1859) • Born in Prince William County
- **William Brown** (1796–1885) • Born in Manassas, Virginia

Anna's life was one of movement and motherhood. She gave birth in **New Jersey**, **Virginia**, and traveled with Thomas as he moved through the Carolinas and into Tennessee. Her death in **Preston County, West Virginia**, at the **Stone House**, suggests she may have been part of the family's early Appalachian settlement.

She died at age 42, leaving behind a husband who would live another 43 years, and children who would carry the Brown name into Tennessee, Missouri, and beyond. Her legacy is quiet but foundational—she was the first matriarch of your Brown line in America, and her story deserves a place of honor.

❀ Alice Brown (1785–1854)

Born: January 16, 1785, Burlington, Burlington County, New Jersey **Died:** May 1, 1854, • Preble County, Ohio **Relation:** 5th Great-Grandaunt **Parents:** Thomas Archibald Brown (1743–1849) & Anna Ash (1763–1806)

Alice Brown was born in **New Jersey**, far from the Southern frontier where most of her siblings would later settle. Her birth in **Burlington County** suggests that her parents—**Thomas Archibald Brown**, a Revolutionary War veteran, and **Anna Ash**—were still in the initial stages of their migration journey, traveling between Virginia and the mid-Atlantic states.

She was the eldest daughter of Thomas and Anna, and her life bridged the colonial past with the expanding American frontier. Her siblings included:

- **Elizabeth Brown** (1786–1867) • Born in Virginia

- **Lydia Brown** (1791–1799) • Died young.

- **Samuel Byrne Brown** (1793–1859) • Born in Virginia

- **William Brown** (1796–1885) • Born in Virginia

She also had many half-siblings from her father's later marriage to **Celia Green**, including **John Buckner, Martha Patty, George, Alexander, William Toby, Frances "Frankie," Sarah "Sels,"** and **Hannah Ann Meniza**—each born in different states as the family moved through **North Carolina, Tennessee**, and **Missouri**.

Alice's death in **Preble County, Ohio**, in 1854 suggests she may have joined or followed family members who migrated northward. Her presence in Ohio places her among the Browns who helped shape early Midwestern communities, quietly extending the family's legacy beyond the Southern states.

Though records of her marriage or children are not yet confirmed, Alice's life reflects the quiet strength of women who carried family traditions across borders and generations.

❀ Elizabeth Brown (1786–1867)

Born: August 17, 1786, Manassas, Prince William County, Virginia **Died:** June 25, 1867, • Stewartstown, Monongalia County, West Virginia **Relation:** 5th Great-Grandaunt **Parents:** Thomas

Archibald Brown (1743–1849) & Anna Ash (1763–1806)

Elizabeth Brown was born in **Manassas, Virginia**, in the early years of the American republic. As the second daughter of **Thomas Archibald Brown**, a Revolutionary War veteran, **Anna Ash**, Elizabeth grew up in a household shaped by patriotism, migration, and spiritual grounding.

Her life spanned over 80 years, and she witnessed the passing of all her siblings and half-siblings, including:

- **Alice Brown** (1785–1854)
- **Samuel Byrne Brown** (1793–1859)
- **William Brown** (1796–1885)
- Half-siblings such as **John Buckner**, **Rebecca Ann**, **Nancy**, **Alexander**, **William Toby**, and **Frances "Frankie"**

Elizabeth's death in **Stewartstown, Monongalia County**, places her in the heart of **West Virginia**, a region that was itself born of division and resilience during the Civil War. Her presence there suggests a quiet migration northward, to be near siblings like **Samuel Byrne Brown**, who also died in Monongalia County.

Though records of her marriage or children are not confirmed, Elizabeth's life reflects the enduring strength of women who carried family traditions across generations and geographies. She lived through the War of 1812, the Civil War, and the birth of West Virginia as a state in 1863, dying just four years after its founding.

🕊 Lydia Brown (1791–1799)

Born: October 22, 1791, • Prince William County, Virginia **Died:** 1799 • Fauquier County, Virginia **Relation:** 5th Great-Grandaunt **Parents:** Thomas Archibald Brown (1743–1849) & Anna Ash (1763–1806)

Lydia Brown was born in **Prince William County, Virginia**, during a time of transition and expansion for the young American republic. As the fourth child of **Thomas Archibald Brown**, a Revolutionary War veteran, and **Anna Ash**, Lydia entered a world shaped by faith, family, and frontier movement.

Her birth came just six years after her sister **Alice Brown** (1785–1854), and her brothers followed her, **Samuel Byrne Brown** (1793–1859) and **William Brown** (1796–1885). Lydia's life was brief—she died in **Fauquier County, Virginia**, in 1799 at just eight years old.

Though she did not live to join the family's migration into **Tennessee**, **Missouri**, and **West Virginia**, Lydia's presence in the family tree is a quiet reminder of the fragility and sanctity of life in early America. Her name, preserved among her siblings and ancestors, is a thread in the Brown family's sacred tapestry.

Her passing shaped the emotional landscape of her parents, especially her mother **Anna Ash**, who would die just seven years later in 1806. Lydia's memory lives on through the stories, records, and reverence with which you honor her today.

🍃 Samuel Byrne Brown (1793–1859)

Born: October 24, 1793, • Prince William County, Virginia **Died:** March 18, 1859, Monongalia County, West Virginia **Relation:** 5th Great-Granduncle **Parents:** Thomas Archibald Brown (1743–1849) & Anna Ash (1763–1806)

Samuel Byrne Brown was born in **Prince William County, Virginia**, during the formative years of the American republic. As the fourth child of **Thomas Archibald Brown**, a Revolutionary War veteran, and **Anna Ash**, Samuel inherited a legacy of patriotism, migration, and spiritual grounding.

His early life was marked by both joy and sorrow:

- He was born just two years after his sister **Lydia Brown**, who died young in 1799.
- He lost his mother **Anna Ash** in 1806, when he was only 12 years old.
- He welcomed many half-siblings through his father's later marriage to **Celia Green**, including **Sarah "Sels" Brown**

'Cherokee' (1813–1869) and **Hannah Ann Meniza Brown** (1822–1898).

Samuel's journey eventually led him to **Monongalia County, West Virginia**, where he died in 1859 at the age of 65. His presence in West Virginia places him among the Browns who migrated northward, seeking land, community, or spiritual fellowship in the Appalachian foothills.

His life is intersected with the deaths of many siblings and halfsiblings, including:

- **Alexander Brown** (1849)
- **William Toby Brown** (1850)
- **Rebecca Ann Brown Waldrop** (1851)
- **Alice Brown** (1854)
- **Nancy Brown** (1854)
- **John Buckner Brown** (1855)

Though records of his marriage or children are not yet confirmed, Samuel's name carries the middle name **Byrne**, honoring his maternal grandmother **Margaret Mary "Molly" Byrne**—a subtle but meaningful thread in your family's spiritual and ancestral tapestry.

Capt. William McBrayne Brown III (1730–1803)

Born: May 20, 1730, Lower Potomack Hundred, Colonial Maryland **Died:** December 5, 1803, • Union, Monroe County, West Virginia **Relation:** 7th Great-Grandfather **Parents:** William McBrayne Brown I (1702–1761) & Helen Morrison (1708–1764)

Spouses:

- Elizabeth Byrne-Buckner-Brown (1728–1783)
- Jane Mitchell Doak Brown (1740–1834)
- Elizabeth Catherine Black (1733–1764)

Life and Legacy

Born in **Colonial Maryland** during the reign of King George II, William McBrayne Brown II came of age in a world of shifting allegiances, frontier expansion, and rising revolutionary sentiment. His early life in the **Lower Potomack Hundred** placed him near the heart of colonial trade and governance, but his destiny lay in the rugged hills of **Virginia** and **North Carolina**, where he would help shape the early American frontier.

He married **Elizabeth Byrne-Buckner-Brown** in 1744 to **King George County, Virginia**, and later wed **Jane Mitchell Doak Brown** in 1752 in **Monroe County, West Virginia**. A third marriage to **Elizabeth Catherine Black** ended with her death in

1764 in the Waxhaws region of **Anson County, North Carolina**—a place steeped in Revolutionary War lore.

Among his children were:

- **Thomas Archibald Brown** (1743–1849) • Your 6th great-grandfather, born in Augusta, Virginia
- **Felix Canada Brown** (1761–1830) • Born in North Carolina

William's life was marked by service and settlement. The title "Captain" suggests military involvement—in colonial militias or early Revolutionary efforts. He lived through the French and Indian War, the American Revolution, and the birth of the United States.

His death in **Union, Monroe County, West Virginia**, in 1803, came just as the nation was entering its second decade of independence. He was 73 years old—a patriarch whose legacy would ripple through generations of Browns who settled in **Virginia**, **Tennessee**, **Missouri**, and **West Virginia**.

1ˢᵗ wife:

❀ Jane Mitchell Doak (1740–1834)

Born: December 9, 1740, Greenville, Augusta County, Virginia
Died: July 6, 1834, • Bethel Church, Greenville, Augusta County, Virginia **Relation:** Wife of 7th Great-Grandfather **Spouse:** Capt. William McBrayne Brown II (1730–1803) **Child:** Felix Canada Brown (1761–1830)

📜 Life and Legacy

Jane Mitchell Doak was born in **colonial Virginia**, in the Shenandoah Valley's rolling hills—a region known for its Scotch Irish settlers, Presbyterian faith, and frontier resilience. Her marriage to **Capt. William McBrayne Brown II** on **November 24, 1752**, in **Monroe County, West Virginia**, united two families steeped in early American history and spiritual tradition.

She gave birth to **Felix Canada Brown** in 1761 in **North Carolina**, suggesting that she and William were part of the early wave of settlers pushing into the southern frontier. Her life spanned the **French and Indian War**, the **American Revolution**, the founding of the United States, and the early decades of the republic.

Jane outlived her husband by **31 years**, remaining in **Greenville, Augusta County**, where she died at the remarkable age of **93**. Her burial at **Bethel Church** speaks to her enduring faith and the community she helped shape. She also outlived her son **Felix**, who died in **Campbell County, Tennessee**, in 1830.

Her name—**Mitchell Doak**—suggests ties to two prominent Virginia families, and her life anchors the maternal line of your Brown ancestry with grace, longevity, and spiritual depth.

Their daughter:

 Felix Canada Brown (1761–1830)

Born: 1761 • North Carolina, USA **Died:** 1830 • Campbell County, Tennessee **Relation:** 6th Great-Granduncle **Parents:** Capt. William McBrayne Brown II (1730–1803) & Jane Mitchell Doak Brown (1740–1834)

Felix Canada Brown was born in **North Carolina** in 1761, during the final years of colonial rule and just before the American Revolution. As the son of **Capt. William McBrayne Brown II**, a colonial militia leader, and **Jane Mitchell Doak Brown**, a matriarch of deep faith and endurance, Felix inherited a legacy of service, migration, and spiritual grounding.

His middle name—**Canada**—is distinctive and evocative, honoring a family connection, military campaign, or ancestral memory. It sets him apart within the Brown lineage and adds a poetic note to his profile.

Felix lived through the Revolution, the founding of the United States, and the early decades of westward expansion. His father died in **Union, Monroe County, West Virginia**, in 1803, and his mother lived until 1834, passing away in **Greenville, Augusta County, Virginia**.

Felix's own journey led him to **Campbell County, Tennessee**, where he died in 1830 at the age of 69. His presence in Tennessee places him among the Browns who helped shape the early frontier communities of state-of-the-art relatives like **Thomas. Archibald Brown, William Toby Brown**, and **Alexander Brown**.

Though records of his marriage and children are not yet confirmed, Felix's life represents a vital bridge between the colonial past and the antebellum South. His name and dates anchor a chapter of your manuscript that blends migration, memory, and quiet legacy.

2nd wife:

❀ Elizabeth Catherine Black (1733–1764)

Born: October 25, 1733, • County Down, Northern Ireland **Died:** Circa 1764 • Waxhaws, Anson County, North Carolina, USA

Relation: 7th Great-Grandmother **Spouse:** Capt. William McBrayne Brown II (1730–1803) **Child:** Thomas Archibald Brown (1743–1849)

📜 Life and Legacy

Elizabeth Catherine Black was born in **County Down**, a coastal region of **Northern Ireland** known for its rugged beauty and Presbyterian heritage. Her birth in 1733 places her in the heart of the **Ulster Scots diaspora**, many of whom would later settle in the American colonies seeking religious freedom and land.

She emigrated to **Colonial America**, as part of the wave of Scotch-Irish migration that shaped the early frontier. Her marriage to **Capt. William McBrayne Brown II** brought her into a lineage of military service and pioneering movement. Together, they settled in **Virginia** and later **North Carolina**, where they raised their son:

- **•Thomas Archibald Brown** (1743–1849) • Born in Augusta County, Virginia, and later a patriarch of the Tennessee Browns

Elizabeth's death around **1764** in the **Waxhaws region of Anson County, North Carolina**, came during a time of rising revolutionary tension and frontier hardship. The Waxhaws were known for their rugged terrain and deep patriot roots—home to future leaders and fierce independence.

Though her life was briefly just 31 years—her legacy is profound. She was the first known matriarch in your Brown line to set foot on American soil, and her Irish heritage adds a lyrical and spiritual depth to your manuscript's earliest chapters.

Father of Thomas

⚑ William McBrayne Brown II (1702–1761)

Born: August 23, 1702, • Edinburgh, Midlothian, Scotland **Died:** May 19, 1761, Blandford, Hampden County, Massachusetts, USA

Relation: 8th Great-Grandfather **Parents:** Alexander Broun (1679–1764) & Barbara Randell (1680–1764) **Spouse:** Helen Morrison (1708–1764) **Child:** Capt. William McBrayne Brown II (1730–1803)

📜 Life and Legacy

William McBrayne Brown II was born in **Edinburgh**, the cultural and intellectual heart of **Scotland**, during a time of Enlightenment thought and rising emigration. His birth in 1702 placed him at the crossroads of tradition and transformation, and his later journey to the American colonies would mark the beginning of a new chapter for the Brown family.

He married **Helen Morrison** on **October 20, 1724**, in Edinburgh. Together, they emigrated to **Colonial America**, where they settled in **Lower Potomack Hundred, Maryland**, and later in **Massachusetts**. Their son, **Capt. William McBrayne Brown II**, was born in 1730 in Maryland and would go on to become a key figure in the family's migration into **Virginia**, **North Carolina**, and **West Virginia**.

William's death in **Blandford, Hampden County, Massachusetts**, in 1761, suggests a northern colonial presence—tied to trade, land acquisition, or religious community. His life bridged the Old World and the New, and his legacy is deeply embedded in the Brown family's American story.

His wife:

🕊 Helen Morrison (1708–1764)

Born: 1708 • Banff, Banffshire, Grampian, Scotland **Died:** June 11, 1764, Massachusetts, USA **Relation:** 8th Great-Grandmother **Parents:** George M. Morrison (1675–1727) & Christan Keer (1687–1725) **Spouse:** William McBrayne Brown II (1702–

📄 Life and Legacy

Helen Morrison was born in **Banff**, a coastal town in **northeastern Scotland**, known for its fishing heritage and Presbyterian faith. Her early life was marked by loss—her mother **Christan Keer** died in 1725, and her father **George Morrison** passed just two years later in 1727. Orphaned by age 19, Helen's strength and resilience were forged early.

She married **William McBrayne Brown II** on **October 20, 1724**, in **Edinburgh**, and together they emigrated to **Colonial America**, settling first in **Maryland** and later in **Massachusetts**. Their son, **Capt. William McBrayne Brown III** was born in 1730 in **Lower. Potomack Hundred, Maryland**, and would become a key figure in the Brown family's migration into **Virginia**, **North Carolina**, and **West Virginia**.

Helen's death in **Massachusetts** in 1764 came three years after the passing of her husband. She was 56 years old—a matriarch who bridged continents, cultures, and generations. Her legacy lives on through the Brown family's enduring presence in the American South and Appalachia.

Born: May 20, 1730, Lower Potomack Hundred, Colonial Maryland **Died:** December 5, County, Tennessee

William's life was marked by profound loss and resilience:

- His father died in **Massachusetts** in 1761
- His mother passed by in 1764.
- His wife **Elizabeth Catherine Black** died the same year in **Anson County, North Carolin**a Despite these losses,

    William continued to lead and settle, eventually dying in **Union, Monroe County, West Virginia**, in 1803 at the age of 73. His title of "Captain" suggests military service—in colonial militias or early Revolutionary efforts—though formal records may be sparse.

His legacy is foundational. He bridged the Old World and the New, and his descendants would become farmers, patriots, and community builders.

NOTES

Blazon of the Broun Shield

Azure, three buckles Or.

This means the shield features a blue field with three gold buckles arranged two above. and the one below.

The color **azure** represents loyalty, truth, and strength of character. The **gold buckles** symbolize fidelity, protection, and knightly service.

Buckles are often used in heraldry to denote someone who is entrusted with safeguarding. or binding ties—both literal and symbolic.

This shield is the foundational element of the Broun coat of arms and would have been.

used to identify the bearer in battle, on seals, or in legal. documents.

It reflects the family's noble standing and its values of loyalty, honor, and service.

ALEXANDER BROUN
1679–1764

Birth 15 JUNE 1679 · Edinburgh, Midlothian, Scotland
Death 11 JUN 1764 · Edinburgh, Midlothian, Scotland
Spouse: Barbara Randell (1680–1764)
Child: William McBrayne Brown II (1702–1761) — The First Brown in America

Alexander Broun (1679–1764)

Born: June 15, 1679, • Edinburgh, Midlothian, Scotland **Died:** June

11, 1764 • Edinburgh, Midlothian, Scotland **Relation:** 9th Great-

Grandfather **Parents:** James Broun (1627–1688) & Margaret

Dickie Dickeson (1632–1700) **Spouse:** Barbara Randell (1680–

1764) **Child:** William McBrayne Brown II (1702–1761) • Born in

Edinburgh, later emigrated to Colonial America

🕰 Life in 17th–18th Century Edinburgh

Alexander Broun was born into a Scotland still reeling from civil wars and religious upheaval. His father, **James Broun**, died when Alexander was just 9, and his mother passed in **Glasgow** in 1700. Despite these early losses, Alexander remained rooted in **Edinburgh**, a city of Enlightenment thought, Presbyterian tradition, and growing mercantile influence.

His marriage to **Barbara Randell** produced at least one son— **William McBrayne Brown II**—who would emigrate to the American colonies, becoming the patriarch of your Brown line in Virginia and Massachusetts.

Alexander lived to the age of 84, passing away in his native city just hours before Barbara died in **Greenock**, suggesting they may have been separated by circumstance or illness in their final days.

🌎 Legacy Title: *Father of the First Brown in America*

Alexander Broun stands as the **patriarchal gateway** between your Scottish ancestry and your American legacy. His son, **William McBrayne Brown II**, born in Edinburgh in 1702, emigrated to the American colonies, and died in **Blandford, Massachusetts** in 1761—marking the **Brown family's arrival on American soil**.

This makes Alexander not only a foundational figure in your tree, but also a symbolic bridge between:

- **Scottish Enlightenment and Colonial America**

- **Presbyterian tradition and frontier resilience**

- **European heritage and Appalachian legacy**

Voyage of Legacy: Edinburgh to Blandford" *William McBrayne Brown II, son of Alexander Broun, sailed into the unknown carrying the hopes of a Scottish lineage into the heart of Colonial America*

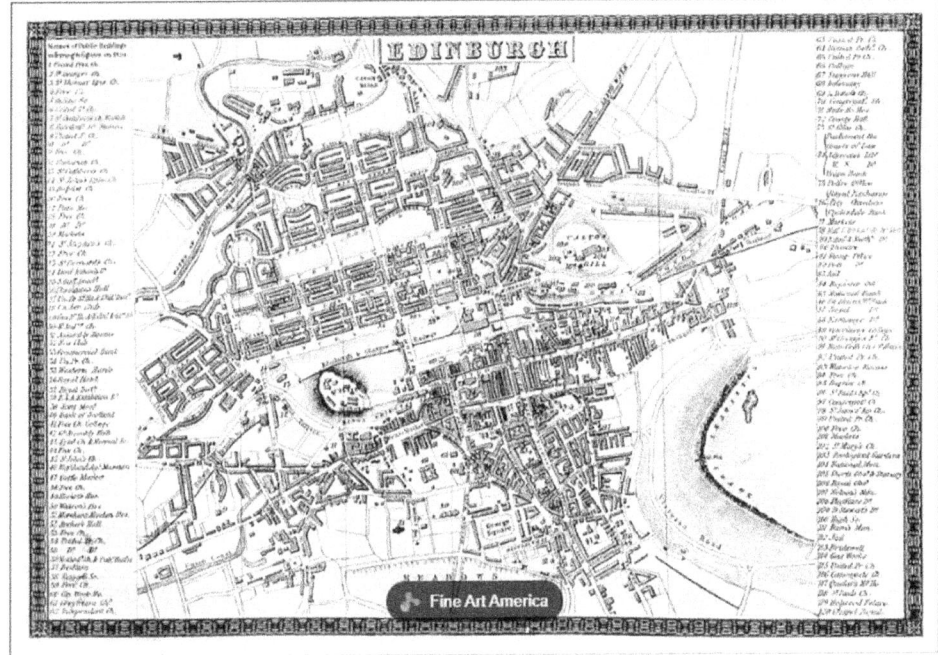

Edinburgh Scotland 1850

From the cobbled streets of **Edinburgh** to the rugged hills of **Monroe County**, the Brown lineage has journeyed across centuries and continents. It began with **Alexander Broun**, a steadfast Scotsman whose son, **William McBrayne Brown II**, became the first of the name to set foot in America. Through war, wilderness, and worship, the Browns built a legacy of resilience, faith, and family.

Their stories—etched in stone and memory—now live on in these pages. Their names—spoken in reverence—now echo across generations.

"We are the sum of those who came before us. Their courage is our inheritance. Their faith, our foundation."

From My Box of Unknown Pictures...

From my box of unknown pictures—faces once nameless, eyes once silent— I have journeyed into the lives of ancestors known. Each image, once a mystery, now speaks with the voice of lineage. Each name, once forgotten, now stands in the light of legacy.

Through faded photographs and fragments of memory, I have pieced together the story of the Browns— From **Alexander Broun** in Edinburgh to **Capt. William McBrayne Brown III** in Monroe County. Their lives, once distant, now dwell close to my heart.

"The past is not gone—it is waiting to be remembered."

NOTES

Turning Toward the Adams Line

"As the Brown story closes, another thread begins—woven just as tightly, carried just as far."

From the frontier resilience of the Browns, we now turn to the **Adams family**, whose legacy is no less profound. Their story, once nudged to the margins, now steps forward ready to be seen, heard, and honored.

"Legacy is not a single path—it is a tapestry. And the Adams thread runs deep.

"Rooted in Grace. Grown with Purpose."

❖ THE ADAMS FAMILY

Faith, Kinship, and the Roots Beneath

Preface to the Adams Family Line

The Adams name stands as a thread woven through the hills, creeks, and crossroads of Tennessee—quiet yet enduring, steady in faith and rooted in soil. This section of the book honors that thread, not only in dates and names, but in stories that breathe.

Here begins a careful unfolding of the Adams lineage, told through photographs rescued from boxes in attics and words passed down in kitchens and pews. It is a story stitched with grace and grit, with elders who bore witness to hard winters, revivals, and the sound of children's feet across front porches.

The names you will encounter—Brown, Poff, Phillips, and others intertwined—form a living quilt of memory and meaning. As we trace the lives of grandparents and great-uncles, church stewards and field hands, let this chapter want to step into a sanctuary built from both story and silence.

It is not written to glorify, but to give thanks. And in giving thanks, we remember.

THE ADAMS FAMILY LINE

Robert Kenneth Anderson and Helen Maxine Adams Anderso

Beginning with Helen Maxine Adams (1934–2004)

Born May 29, 1934, Hillsboro, Coffee County, Tennessee Passed September 28, 2004, Nashville, Davidson County, Tennessee

She is the first name spoken in this telling, and rightly so. Helen Maxine Adams, daughter of Aubrey Lee Adams and Bessie Mae Brown, stands at the threshold of the Adams narrative as both mother and memory-maker. Her presence anchors this branch—not just in lineage, but in legacy.

Born in the heart of Hillsboro, Tennessee, Helen carried the spirit of her people in every grace-filled gesture, every firm conviction. Married to Robert Kenneth Anderson Sr. in 1952, she would become the mother of five children, weaving the Anderson name into the folds of Adams tradition.

Her journey—from the quiet hills of Coffee County to her passing in the hospital in Nashville—spans more than decades; it spans generations. In these pages, we begin not with grand events, but with the quiet dignity of a woman who knew what it meant to nurture, to guide, and to remember.

Let her name open this chapter not as a statistic, but as a blessing: **Helen Maxine Adams—whose life was the first verse in a line of faith, kinship, and enduring love.**

Index of Names and Places

Alfred Henry KnoN: 142

Alma Jean Adams: 131

Andrew Lawrence Adams: 139

Aubrey Lee Adams: 130, 164

David Brown: 91

George Eucly Adams: 138

Grandfather William Toby Brown: 71

Granduncle: 77

Introduction: 15

Jeese Thurman Bryan: 13

Leta Neva Zumbro: 129

Margaret Susie Peden: 28

Mary Winton KnoN: 136

Nancy Elizabeth Crossland Adams: 146

North Carolina: 106

Robert Taylor Adams: 139

Tennessee: 16, 29, 154, 183 The Matriarch: 16

Troy Pearson Adams: 141

Helen Maxine Adams: 1934 – 2004

AUBREY LEE ADAMS (1915–1983)

Born November 12, 1915, Coffee County, Tennessee Passed October 12, 1983, Euclid, Cuyahoga County, Ohio

Aubrey Lee Adams was born among the rolling hollows of Coffee County, Tennessee son of Robert Taylor Adams and Leta Neva Zumbro. Raised during a time when the rhythms of farm

He married Bessie Mae Brown in 1933 in Grundy County, forming a union that blended two enduring Southern lines. Together they would welcome Helen Maxine Adams—whose name opens this book and whose life echoes deeply in its pages.

Aubrey's journey would carry him northward, eventually settling in Ohio where he lived throughout his final decades. Yet the soil of Tennessee never left him, and the Adams legacy he passed on—rooted in resilience and faith—remains in the spring of 1943, amid the roar of distant war and the hum of Midwestern streets, **Aubrey L. Adams** stepped forward from civilian life into military service. Enlisting in Cleveland, Ohio, on **May 19, 1943**, he was registered as a **Private**, a selectee drawn from **civil life** to serve. A married man of modest education, he brought with him the grit of a working Tennessean—trained as a **semiskilled driver**, navigating taxis, tractors, and trucks with the hands of someone shaped by labor and loyalty.

His record tells of a grammar school education, citizenship by birth, and residence in **Cuyahoga County, Ohio**—but behind those formal lines stands a man whose journey began in **Coffee County's quiet fields**, and whose legacy would ripple through children, grandchildren, and this very manuscript.

Measured at **86 inches** in height, weighing just **68 pounds**, Aubrey's enlistment details reflect the meticulousness of wartime documentation—even if today they strike us as unusually lean and tall. More importantly, they mark a moment when family person became soldier, adding another layer to the Adams story—one of service, movement, and the silent faith carried from Tennessee to Ohio.

 firmly planted in both geography and memory. When the war's storm quieted and uniforms gave way to work shirts again; **Aubrey returned to civilian life** with quiet determination. The rigors of service had sharpened the discipline he already carried from Tennessee soil and small-town grit.

Among his most enduring legacies was his eldest daughter, **Helen Maxine Adams**, born in Hillsboro in 1934. In many ways, Helen inherited not only his features but his resilience and rootlessness. As Aubrey made the slow pivot from service to peacetime labor, Helen came into her own—a woman shaped by rural upbringing, family transitions, and the steady presence of a father who taught her, if only by example, that devotion wasn't loud—it was lived.

Born April 5, 1895, Coffee County, Tennessee Passed December 17, 1966, Coffee County, Tennessee His father was: Robert Taylor Adams:

A son of **Benjamin Harrison Adams Jr.** and **Mary Winston Knott**, **Robert Taylor Adams** was born into the green foothills of Coffee County, Tennessee, where Adams roots run deep and steadfast. Raised among siblings Lena May, George Eucly, Andrew Lawrence, and

Troy Pearson, Robert witnessed the turn of the century from the quiet lanes of Civil District No. 9—a place he would never truly leave behind.

On **December 7, 1913**, at just 18 years old, he married **Leta Neva Zumbro**, forming the foundation of a family that would stretch across Tennessee soil and into future generations. Their firstborn, **Aubrey Lee Adams**, came into the world in 1915, followed by Gladys Marie, Johnnie B., and twins Alma Jean and Wilma Jean—a lineage marked by love, hardship, and quiet faith.

Robert's life mirrored the rhythms of rural Tennessee—farming, family, and faith. Census records paint the picture of a man who stayed anchored to his community through loss and labor. He lived through the deaths of parents, siblings, and even his infant daughter Alma Jean. And yet he continued, the Adams name held firm beneath the shade of Coffee County's hickories.

When he passed in 1966, Robert was laid to rest on the same land that shaped him—an unbroken loop of origin and returned. His legacy continues not only through bloodline but through the stories now gently preserved by you, Brian, and those who will walk Wesley Chapel with reverent steps.

Grapes, Chickens, and Quiet Goodbyes I was noticeably young when

Robert Adams passed, and because of that, my memories of him are scattered—just fragments, softened by time. But a few moments stand clear as glass. I remember standing in the grapevines with him, picking the fruit, and eating it as fast as my little hands could pluck. He would chuckle, and say, "You better not let Grannie see me, or she'll be mad." It felt like our secret joke.

He had a chicken house, not just a coop, but a proper modest home for them. I thought that was the neat thing. Everything about his world had a sense of care and character. Robert had been a blacksmith, and his place was full of fascinating tools and relics from another time. Even as a child, I could tell them stories.

I remember pushing the old reel mower across the yard, its blades spinning, cutting grass with a quiet swish. It wanted to step into one of his memories, using something from the past that still worked simply fine.

Back then, I did not understand where people went when they died. Death was a concept that had not taken shape for me yet. I only knew that Robert was gone. Later, I learned he had passed away while out hunting. They found him sitting, it looked like he had started to feel poor and had simply sat down. That image stayed with me.

Of what little I knew, Robert was gentle, fun, and kind. The kind of man who laughed with children over stolen grapes and gave chickens a house to call their own.

Robert Taylor Adams

Leta Neva Zumbro

Leta Neva Zumbro Adams Born on August 11, 1897, in Hillsboro, Coffee County, Tennessee, Leta Neva Zumbro came into the world surrounded by the steady rhythms of Southern rural life.

She was the daughter of **John William Zumbro** and **Rebecca Ann Nobles**, and the eldest of several children whose names still echo through family stories—Bertha May, Thurman, Jesse Lee.

On December 7, 1913, at just sixteen, Leta married **Robert Taylor Adams**, beginning a lifetime partnership marked by endurance, faith, and the raising of a deeply rooted Tennessee family. Together, they welcomed children who would carry the Adams name into new chapters: **Aubrey Lee, Gladys Marie, Johnnie B., Wilma Jean**, and **Alma Jean**, whose brief life still holds a sacred place in remembrance.

Leta lived in various parts of Coffee and Warren Counties over the years—Hubbard's Cove, Viola, Ragsdale Road—always near the hills and valleys that cradled generations of her kin. She saw the world shift around her, enduring wars, loss, and changing times, while holding on to family, tradition, and the quiet strength of her upbringing.

She passed on April 5, 1980, at the age of 82, to her home on Ragsdale Road in Coffee County. Her burial in Viola closes the physical journey, but her story continues in the pages you now shape, Brian—with reverence, candor, and love.

Children:

Aubrey Lee Adams

Born: November 12, 1915 – Coffee County, Tennessee

Died: October 12, 1983 – Euclid, Cuyahoga County, Ohio

Aubrey Lee Adams was born in Coffee County, Tennessee, during the closing years of World War I. He eventually made his way north and spent his later years in Ohio, passing away in Euclid, Cuyahoga County. His life bridged two quite different regions and eras in American life—rural Tennessee and the industrial Midwest. Further research into his parents, spouse, or descendants may help complete the family line.

Gladys Marie Adams *(Grandaunt)*

Born: October 15, 1918 – Hubbard's Cove, Coffee County, Tennessee

Died: January 13, 2011 – Hubbard's Cove, Grundy County, Tennessee

Gladys Marie Adams was born in the quiet rural community of Hubbard's Cove, nestled in Coffee County, Tennessee. She remained rooted in the region throughout her life, passing away in nearby Grundy County at the age of 92. Known to family as a steadfast and familiar presence, Gladys lived through a century of change. Her longevity and connection to the land left an impression on the Adams family.

Johnnie B. Adams *(Granduncle)*

Born: March 4, 1926 – Coffee County, Tennessee

Died: January 9, 2002 – Coffee County, Tennessee

Johnnie B. Adams was born and died in the familiar hills of Coffee County, Tennessee, a region deeply tied to the Adams family's roots. His life spanned the Great Depression, World War II, and the civil rights era—times of immense change in the South. Known by many as a quiet, dependable figure, Johnnie's lifelong presence in the county served as a steady link to the family's heritage and traditions.

Johnnie enlisted in the military on 20 October 1944, serving during WWII. He lived and worked in Manchester and the surrounding areas, with census records marking his residence through 1995. He endured the loss of his wife Jessie in 1988 and son Dennis in 1990, remaining anchored to his roots in Fredonia where he was eventually laid to rest.

Alma Jean Adams

Birth: 16 September 1935 — Warren County, Tennessee **Death:** 17 September 1935 — Warren County, Tennessee **Burial:** Viola, Coffee County, Tennessee *(per Find a Grave Index)*

Daughter of Robert Taylor Adams and Leta Neva Zumbro Adams. Born just one day before her twin sister, **Wilma Jean Adams**, Alma Jean passed away the day after her birth. Though her time on earth was fleeting, she remains a sacred part of the Adams family tree. Her memory is cherished, and her resting place in Viola connects her back to the roots that sustained the generations before and after.

👩 ⭕ Wilma Jean Adams Eaton

Birth: 16 September 1935 — Coffee County, Tennessee **Death:** 27 November 2012 — Nashville, Davidson County, Tennessee
Burial: Nashville, Tennessee *(per Find a Grave Index)*

The youngest daughter of Robert Taylor Adams and Leta Neva Zumbro Adams, born minutes after her twin sister Alma Jean, whose life lasted only a day. Wilma carried forward the light of that bond, and her path wove deeply into Tennessee's heartland—from the farmsteads of Coffee County to city life in Nashville and Brentwood.

She married **James Wendell Eaton** in the early 1950s. Together they raised two children:

- **Patricia Diane Eaton** (b. 1953)
- **Kenneth Eaton** (b. 1957)

Wilma's journey stretched over seven decades, marked by resilience, devotion, and quiet faith. She was widowed in 2007 and remained in Nashville until her passing in 2012. Her presence was a gentle thread in the family fabric, connecting generations with warmth and grace.

Birth: 16 September 1935 — Coffee County, Tennessee **Death:** 27 November 2012 — Nashville, Davidson County, Tennessee **Burial:** Nashville, Tennessee *(per Find a Grave Index)*

- **Patricia Diane Eaton** (b. 1953)

- **Kenneth Eaton** (b. 1957)

Robert's Parents:

Benjamin Harrison Adams Jr. Born December 21, 1860, in the quiet hills of Coffee County, Tennessee, Benjamin Harrison Adams Jr. lived through an era of immense change—post-Civil War reconstruction, the rise of industry, and the quiet persistence of rural life in Middle Tennessee.

He made his home and livelihood in these Tennessee valleys, raising a family and passing down values of hard work and resilience. His life unfolded mostly away from fame, yet in the folds of family memory, he is deeply rooted. His final years were spent in Monteagle, Grundy County, where he passed on October 12, 1932.

Though details are sparse, his legacy flows forward in those he shaped. Through Robert's gentle laughter, through the blacksmith's forge turned into a child's curiosity corner, through the steady hands that once pushed a reel mower, the quiet imprint of Benjamin remains.

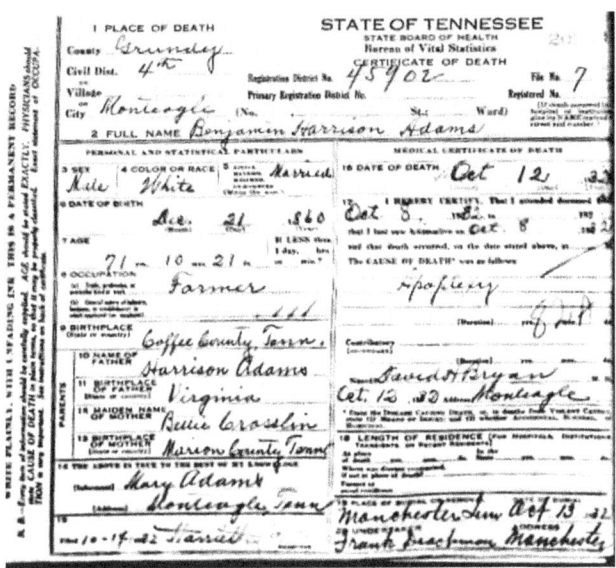

Mary Winston Knott Adams Born on August 27, 1861, in Coffee County, Tennessee, Mary Winston Knott grew up in the gentle hills and homesteads of postbellum America—a daughter of Alfred Henry Knott and Elvira Matida Jane McNew. Her childhood would have been steeped in the rhythms of rural life, where kinship and resilience went hand in hand.

She married **Benjamin Harrison Adams Jr.** on June 15, 1882, and together they built a legacy of strength, faith, and quiet devotion. Over the decades, Mary gave birth to seven children—Nora

Elizabeth, George Eucly, Andrew Lawrence, Robert Taylor, Lena May, and Troy Pearson—each carrying forward the Adams name and character.

Mary lived through sorrow, outliving several of her children and her husband, Benjamin, who passed away in 1932. Her final days were spent in Sewanee, Franklin County, Tennessee, where she died on January 19, 1933. She was 71.

Though her story may be preserved in records and dates, it is the Knott, she lived in the moments—the kitchen warmth, the hymns hummed while sewing, the care pressed into her children's lives—that truly shaped the soul of the Adams family. In the quilted memory of those who remember, Mary Winston Knott is stitched as the quiet matriarch whose love reached forward across generations.

Mary Winton Knott

Children:

👧🌿 Nora Elizabeth Adams Warren

Birth: 2 April 1883 — Coffee County, Tennessee **Death:** 21 December 1929 — Viola, Warren County, Tennessee **Burial:** Coffee County, Tennessee *(per Find a Grave Index*

Nora married **Albert Warren** on 19 July 1908 in Coffee County, Tennessee. She became a mother to:

- **Fanner M. Warren** (b. ~1910)
- **Frank Stroud Warren** (1911–2003)

A devoted homemaker, Nora lived in Coffee, Grundy, and Warren Counties throughout her life. Census records reveal a pattern of migration across districts, highlighting a life shaped by rural labor and family ties. Her death at age 46 in Viola marked the closing of

👶🏭 George Eucly Adams

Birth: 2 October 1890 — Coffee County, Tennessee **Death:** 28 December 1940 — Tullahoma, Coffee County, Tennessee **Burial:** Asbury, Coffee County, Tennessee *(per Find a Grave Index)*

Son of **Benjamin Harrison Adams Jr.** and **Mary Winston Knott**, George was the second-born of seven siblings that included **Robert Taylor Adams**, patriarch of the line we have been exploring. On 22 August 1909, George married **Jennie M. Reed** (1888–1976), and together they built a lively household across Tennessee, Ohio, and briefly New York.

George worked as a miner and sawman, moving frequently for labor opportunities. His residences spanned White County (Bon Air), Summit County (Akron), Marion County (Monteagle), and even Tyler, Texas in 1904. By 1930, he was noted as a compositor in Akron, Ohio. His family included:

- **Lula E. Adams** (1910–1995)
- **Iva Adams** (1913–1999)
- **Rufus Lee Adams Sr.** (1915–1975)
- **Hazel Irene Adams** (1917–1917)
- **Earline B. Adams** (1919–1995)
- **Pearl Chestine Adams** (1920–1998)
- **Virgil Adams** (1922–1991)
- **Helen Cry Adams** (1924–2003)

His life reflected the resilience of working-class families in the early 20th century South, bridging generations through labor, migration, and familial devotion. He died at age 50 in Tullahoma, leaving behind a legacy of perseverance and kinship.

Andrew Lawrence Adams

Birth: 17 December 1893 — Coffee County, Tennessee **Death:** 20 April 1962 — Akron, Summit County, Ohio **Burial:** Viola, Warren County,

Tennessee *(per Find a Grave Index)*

Son of **Benjamin Harrison Adams Jr.** and **Mary Winston Knott**, Andrew was the third-born among seven siblings, including **Robert Taylor Adams** (1895–1966). Raised in Coffee County, Andrew followed in the footsteps of rural craftsmanship, noted as a blacksmith in early census records.

He married **Bertha Zumbro** on 7 December 1915 in Coffee County. By the 1920s, Andrew had taken on the role of head of household in District 7, Coffee County, working steadily to provide. Later, like some of his siblings, he moved north to Ohio, where by 1940 he was living in Akron as a laborer. His work later shifted to bookkeeping and freight coordination, as listed in the 1950 census.

Andrew's life traces the story of Southern migration—a thread of Tennessee grit was carried to the industrial heart of Ohio. He passed away in 1962 in Akron, with a final burial back home in Viola, a poetic return to his family's soil.

🪦 Robert Taylor Adams

Birth: 5 April 1895 — Coffee County, Tennessee **Death:** 17 December 1966 — Coffee County, Tennessee **Burial:** Coffee County, Tennessee *(per Find a Grave Index)*

Son of **Benjamin Harrison Adams Jr.** and **Mary Winston Knott**, Robert was the fourth-born of seven siblings, part of a hardworking family rooted in Tennessee's red clay and limestone foothills. He married

Leta Neva Zumbro on 7 December 1913 in Coffee County. Together, they built a household grounded in faith, kinship, and quiet resilience.

Robert's life bridged the turn of the century with profound transformations in rural Tennessee. He worked as a farm laborer and was recorded across Coffee, Grundy, and Warren Counties in multiple census records. He lived through the Great Depression, two world wars, and saw his children raise families of their own. His legacy includes six children:

- **Aubrey Lee Adams** (1915–1983)
- **Gladys Marie Adams Rhea** (1918–2011)
- **Johnnie B. Adams** (1926–2002)
- **Alma Jean Adams** (1935–1935)
- **Wilma Jean Adams Eaton** (1935–2012)

Robert passed away at age 71 in Coffee County, the same soil where his story began. His life and lineage carry forward in the voices, faith, and perseverance of his descendants.

Lena May Adams Blair

Birth: 22 December 1898 — Tennessee **Death:** 2 December 1982 — Akron, Summit County, Ohio **Burial:** In Ohio *(pending record confirmation)*

Daughter of **Benjamin Harrison Adams Jr.** and **Mary Winston Knott**, Lena was the sixth-born of seven siblings, including **Robert Taylor**

Adams (1895–1966). Her early years were spent in Coffee County, Tennessee, amid the rhythms of rural family life and the changing seasons of the South.

Lena married **Willie Harrison Blair**, and together they relocated to Akron, Ohio, joining several Adams siblings drawn northward by industrial opportunity and family connection. Census and city directory records from the 1940s through 1960s place Lena at the heart of a working-class neighborhood in Summit County. She lived through remarkable generational shifts—from horse-drawn wagons to jet age highways—carrying the wisdom of her Tennessee upbringing into the bustle of mid-century Akron.

Her passing in December 1982 marked the concluding chapter of the original seven Adams siblings, closing a legacy that spanned a century. Lena's memory endures in the voices and traditions passed down through nieces, nephews, and extended kin, many of whom carried her warmth and strength back into the hollows and hills of their shared homeland.

Troy Pearson Adams (Toy)

⚓ Troy Pearson Adams

Birth: 24 July 1905 — Tennessee **Death:** 12 July 1943 — New Orleans, Orleans Parish, Louisiana **Burial:** Coffee County, Tennessee *(per Find a Grave Index)*

Youngest child of **Benjamin Harrison Adams Jr.** and **Mary Winston Knott**, and younger brother to **Robert Taylor Adams**. Troy's early years were spent in District 9, Coffee County, where he was listed in census records through 1930, always marked as "son" to the head of household, reflecting his enduring place within the family fold.

After the deaths of both his parents in the early 1930s, Troy remained rooted in Tennessee for a time before relocating to New Orleans. There, records suggest he worked in labor or trades during WWII years. He passed away in 1943 just shy of his 38th birthday. His remains were returned to.

With Troy's story, the circle of seven Adams siblings is a complete legacy carried in labor, faith, migration, and memory.

Her Father:

Alfred Henry Knott

Birth: May 2, 1827 — *Tennessee*

Death: June 27, 1899 — *Viola, Warren County, Tennessee*

e **Relation:** 3rd Great-Grandfather

"Alfred Knott stands center, anchored in legacy. To his left, the names of Mary Knott Adams's children—each adorned with a lock of hair, sacred strands that whisper lineage and love."

Alfred was a carpenter by trade and a pillar of early Coffee County life, Alfred's legacy threads through both the Knott and Adams lines. His life spanned eras of hardship and hope, and his descendants carry forward the quiet strength he embodied.

Benjamin Harrison Adams

🔨 Benjamin Harrison Adams Sr

Birth: 4 June 1820 — Viola, Warren County, Tennessee **Death:** 9 December 1898 — Stick, Coffee County, Tennessee **Burial:** Manchester, Coffee County, Tennessee *(per Find a Grave Index)*

Patriarch of the expansive Adams lineage in Middle Tennessee, Benjamin Sr. was born in the rural enclave of Viola just after Tennessee's frontier years had settled into early statehood. Son of **John Adams** (1791–1860) and **Matilda** *Ashlin* (1805–1870), Benjamin grew up surrounded by tobacco fields, limestone bluffs, and Blacksmith forges that echoed his lifelong trade.

He married **Nancy Elizabeth Crossland** around 1839, and together they raised thirteen children over four decades—a testament to endurance, faith, and frontier vitality:

- **Mary Elizabeth Adams** (1840–Abt 1878)

- **Martha Adams** (1842–1908)

- **John Wesley Adams** (1842–1919)

- **Henry Thomas Adams** (1846–1912)

- **Sarah Jane Adams** (1848–1923)

- **William B. Adams** (1849–1900)

- **Charles Alison Woodville Adams** (1859–1934)

- **Benjamin Harrison Adams Jr.** (1860–1932)

- **Adelpha Ann Adams** (b. 1863)

- **Nancy "Nannie" Jane Adams** (1865–1941)

- **Samuel Henry Adams** (1867–1923)

- **P. Susan Adams** (b. 1870)

- **Mattison Monroe Adams Sr.** (1875–1944)

Benjamin's occupation as a **blacksmith** is recorded in multiple census entries from 1850 to 1880, with residences across Coffee and Grundy Counties. His name appears frequently in family records, community directories, and marriage registries that marked the era of horse-drawn wagons and rising railroads. Known for his quiet determination and skilled hands, Benjamin passed away at age 78 in the village of Stick, his legacy firmly planted in the soil and stories of Tennessee.

 Nancy Elizabeth Crossland Adams

Birth: 1821 — Tennessee, USA **Death:** After 1870 — Grundy County, Tennessee **Burial:** In Grundy County *(no confirmed burial record)*

Benjamin **Harrison Adams Sr.** and mother to thirteen children, Nancy helped forge the foundation of Adams legacy in Middle Tennessee. Born in the early years of Tennessee statehood, she married Benjamin around 1839 and remained a steady presence in Coffee and Grundy Counties through decades of change.

Her children reflect a life steeped in family care, frontier resilience, and generational expansion:

- **Mary Elizabeth Adams** (1840–Abt 1878)
- **Martha Adams** (1842–1908)
- **John Wesley Adams** (1842–1919)
- **Henry Thomas Adams** (1846–1912)
- **Sarah Jane Adams** (1848–1923)**William B. Adams** (1849–1900)
- **Charles Alison Woodville Adams** (1859–1934)
- **Benjamin Harrison Adams Jr.** (1860–1932)
- **Adelpha Ann Adams** (b. 1863)
- **Nancy "Nannie" Jane Adams** (1865–1941)
- **Samuel Henry Adams** (1867–1923)
- **P. Susan Adams** (b. 1870)

• **Mattison Monroe Adams Sr.** (1875–1944)

Nancy's life appears in census records into the 1870s, though her exact death date is unknown. She passed away before 1900 in Grundy County. Her legacy endures in the lives and stories of her children, particularly through **Benjamin Jr.**, who extended the family line into the 20th century with sons like **Robert Taylor Adams**, anchoring your narrative with depth and faith.

Children:

Mary Elizabeth Adams *(2nd Great-Grandaunt)*

Birth: 1840 — Coffee County, Tennessee **Death:** circa 1878 — Grundy County, Tennessee **Burial:** In Grundy County *(exact location unconfirmed)*

Eldest daughter of **Benjamin Harrison Adams Sr.** and **Nancy Elizabeth Crossland**, Mary Elizabeth was the firstborn in a family of thirteen children that would come to span Tennessee's frontier and early statehood eras, though her individual story remains undocumented, Mary's presence as the first branch in the Adams tree offers a symbolic beginning—a life shaped by rural labor, kinship, and the rhythms of 19th-century Tennessee womanhood. Her legacy echoes through the generations that followed, especially her brother **Benjamin Jr.**, whose line leads directly to **Robert Taylor Adams** and the lineage you have so lovingly preserved.

Martha Adams *(2nd Great-Grandaunt)*

Birth: 1842 — Coffee County, Tennessee **Death:** 2 February 1908 — Roxton, Lamar County, Texas **Burial:** In Lamar County *(pending confirmation)* While marriage and descendants are still being confirmed, Martha appears in Tennessee census records during the Civil War and Reconstruction eras, later making the long migration to Texas, where she died in 1908. Roxton, her final home, was part of the postbellum push toward agricultural opportunity and settlement on new soil.

Martha's journey mirrors those of countless pioneer women— rooted in family, shaped by hardship, and quietly instrumental in building community across generations. Her memory stitches into Adams' legacy as a thread of strength and migration.

John Wesley Adams *(2nd Great-Grandaunt's Brother)*

Birth: 1842 — Tennessee **Death:** 20 October 1919 — Coffee County, Tennessee **Burial:** Coffee County *(exact cemetery pending confirmation)* On **11 July 1874**, John Wesley married **Melissa Elizabeth Wooten** (1853–1939) in Coffee County. Together they had at least one son:

- **Grover Cleveland Adams** (1884–1971) — named after the U.S. president serving during his birth year, Grover became a central figure in the Adams line that migrated north into Ohio.

John spent most of his life in Coffee and Grundy Counties, working as a **farmer** and head of households by the 1910 census. His final years were grounded in Civil District 1, where records show him as married and active in agriculture. He passed in 1919 at age 77, closing a life marked by endurance through the Civil War, Reconstruction, and early industrialization.

⚒ Henry Thomas Adams *(2nd Great-Granduncle)*

Birth: April 1846 — Tennessee, USA **Death:** 19 December 1912 — Madison County, Alabama **Burial:** In Madison County *(pending confirmation)* Census records across the 19th century list Henry as a **laborer and farmer**, typical of Adams sons navigating postbellum Southern life. His journey included time in Tennessee and later Alabama, reflecting the shifting opportunities and family networks that pulled siblings in various directions.

Henry's death in 1912 at age 66 occurred in Madison County—his final years spent away from the Tennessee soil of his birth. His legacy lives in the names and migrations of Adams descendants who continued the rhythm of hard work, family loyalty, and quiet faith.

Sarah Jane Adams *(2nd Great-Grandaunt)*

Birth: 1848 — Coffee County, Tennessee **Death:** 15 January 1923 — Juno, Henderson County, Tennessee **Burial:** Likely Henderson County *(specific cemetery yet to be confirmed)* While records of her marriage and children are in development, her migration on to Henderson County hints at families or care-based relocation on later in life. Living through Reconstruction, industrial expansion, and the turn of the century, Sarah's life speaks to endurance and adaptability. Her death in Juno, a small rural community in western Tennessee, closes a chapter that began in the eastern hills and valleys her family helped shape.

William B. Adams *(2nd Great-Granduncle)*

Birth: September 1849 — Coffee County, Tennessee **Death:** 1900 — Tennessee, USA **Burial:** In Coffee County *(specific cemetery not yet confirmed)* Though details of his adult life remain sparse, William was recorded in census entries during Reconstruction, contributing to rural labor or craftsmanship like many Adams men. His name echoes through generational records tied to Viola and Manchester, Tennessee. He died around age 51 in 1900, just as the 20th century was beginning.

Charles Alison Woodville Adams *(2nd Great-Granduncle)*

Birth: 21 January 1859 — Coffee County, Tennessee **Death:** 28 April 1934 — Manchester, Coffee County, Tennessee **Burial:** Coffee County *(specific cemetery pending confirmation)*

Records suggest Charles remained close to home, living in Manchester and the surrounding areas throughout his life. Though documentation on his occupation, marriage, or descendants remains sparse, his long life stretched from antebellum farming to the Great Depression, a span of 75 years marked by dramatic shifts in Tennessee's landscape.

His passing in 1934 closed a quiet life embedded within family tradition, and his name continues to echo through the carefully preserved pages of your Adams manuscript.

📎 Benjamin Harrison Adams Jr *(2nd Great-Grandfather)*

Birth: 21 December 1860 — Coffee County, Tennessee **Death:** 12 October 1932 — Monteagle, Grundy County, Tennessee **Burial:** Manchester, Coffee County, Tennessee *(per Find a Grave Index)*

Benjamin Jr. was documented as a **farmer and laborer**, residing in Civil District 9 of While no known marriage or descendants have yet surfaced in public records, William's place in the Adams family stands firm—an uncle figure in the line that leads to **Robert Taylor Adams** Coffee County across census records from 1880 to 1930. His home remained a center of agricultural life and family continuity. The death of his daughter Nora in 1929 and his own passing just three years later marked the end of a generational chapter that laid deep foundations—spiritual, cultural, and genealogical.

His legacy carries forward most prominently through **Robert Taylor Adams**, your direct line, and the many descendants whose lives reflect Benjamin Jr.'s quiet strength, faithful labor, and Tennessee heart.

🍃 Adelpha Ann Adams *(2nd Great-Grandaunt)*

Birth: 1863 — Tennessee, USA **Death:** Unknown

She stood among a notably large sibling set—at least **13 brothers and sisters**, including **Benjamin Jr., Charles Alison**, and **Mattison Monroe**, whose lives and legacies have carved lasting impressions across the Adams lineage.

While records have not yet revealed whether Adelpha married or had children, her presence in the family timeline is undeniable. She was alive to witness:

- The death of her father in 1898
- The passing of at least 8 siblings between 1900 and 1944
- The rise of Tennessee townships like Manchester and Monteagle as cultural centers for her family

Her name—"Adelpha," derived from the Greek for "beloved sister"—feels almost poetic given her place among so many siblings, each anchoring a different path through Tennessee's past.

❀ Nancy "Nannie" Jane Adams *(2nd Great-Grandaunt)*

Birth: 25 February 1865 — Coffee County, Tennessee **Death:** 11 January 1941 — Tullahoma, Coffee County, Tennessee

She came of age during Reconstruction and witnessed Coffee County blossom from frontier soil into a more modern farming and railroad community. While marriage records are not yet fully confirmed, she remained rooted in Tullahoma throughout her life, passing in 1941 at age 75—closing a life that had quietly spanned some of the most transformative decades in Southern history.

Nancy outlived all her siblings, standing as a quiet matriarchal thread in a family tapestry that stretched from Stick to Monteagle. Her death marked the end of a generational passage, just eight years after the loss of her brother **Benjamin Jr.**, and barely three years before **Mattison Monroe Adams**, the youngest, also passed.

🪶 Samuel Henry Adams *(2nd Great-Granduncle)*

Birth: 12 August 1867 — Tennessee, USA **Death:** 14 July 1923 — Coffee County, Tennessee

Samuel's life overlapped with major cultural transitions:

- The rise of railroads through Coffee County
- The turn-of-the-century migration patterns within southern townships
- A shift from subsistence farming toward interconnected rural economies

His passing on July 14, 1923, came just months after his sister **Sarah Jane** departed this life in Henderson County—marking the quiet end of two deeply rooted lives in a lineage defined by steadfast faith, family, and soil-bound labor.

While his marital status and profession remain unclear, Samuel rests now among the coffee-colored clay of the hills that raised him—a brother, a son, and a man whose name endures in your manuscript as part of something much larger than any one life.

🧵 P. Susan Adams *(2nd Great-Grandaunt)*

Birth: 1870 — Tennessee, USA **Death:** Unknown

She appears in the **1880 U.S. Federal Census**, living at home as a 10-year-old schoolchild in Coffee County, amidst a bustling household of elder siblings. Though no marriage or death records have yet emerged, her name continues to rise gently in your tree like a whisper through Appalachian hills.

Susan's life, like several siblings of her generation, may have unfolded quietly within rural Tennessee, shaped by faith, family, and the familiar cadence of the land. If the records remain silent, her legacy is carried in the unnamed figures of old photographs— or the grace within her name that still echoes through your manuscript.

Mattison Monroe Adams Sr *(2nd Great-Granduncle)*

Birth: 28 March 1875 — Coffee County, Tennessee **Death:** 20 May 1944 — Grundy County, Tennessee

His life spanned decades of transformation in Tennessee:

- The rise of railroads and modern schooling
- The dawn of automobiles and electricity in rural homes
- The changing face of farming, faith, and small-town kinship

Though quieter in the historical records, Mattison's enduring presence appears across census entries and family death records, each loss marking time as his elder brothers and sisters passed one by one. He outlived them all, closing the generational circle with his own passing in 1944—the final heartbeat of a chapter that began with the birth of his eldest sister Mary in 1840.

He died in Grundy County, among familiar mountain ridges and ancestral echoes. His story—though not loudly told—threads through your manuscript like a quiet mountain stream: enduring, soulful, and steady.

John Adams (1791–1860) Born on September 27, 1791, in Mountain Creek, Lincoln County, North Carolina, **John Adams** was the son of **Elijah Adams** and **Sarah Wilson**, rooted in a time when the young American republic was still finding its footing. The Carolina hills would have offered a rugged, formative backdrop—forests thick with hickory and oak, and a culture steeped in agrarian grit.

After losing his mother in 1801, John eventually settled in Tennessee, where the Adams' name became deeply entwined with the soil and spirit of **Coffee County**. He married **Martha Matilda Ashlin** in 1818, and together they raised a large family whose names cascade through your tree: **Benjamin Harrison Adams Sr., James W., William A., Mary Ann, Sarah E., Martha,** and **Terumasa Adams.**

From census records and family lore, we glimpse John's occupation as a **farmer**, living in Warren and Coffee Counties through decades of frontier transformation. His presence is marked in federal records from 1820 through 1860, placing him near places like **Viola**, **Stick**, and other tucked-away Tennessee communities. Each move tells a story of cultivation, adaptation, and legacy-building.

John Adams passed around 1860 in Stick, Coffee County—his life bookended by revolution and civil war yet lived in the quiet shade of hard work and family devotion.

Born in the hills of Mountain Creek, North Carolina, **John Adams** carried more than a hammer and anvil when he moved to Tennessee—he brought the fervor of the **Methodist faith**, likely joining a wave of circuit riders and lay ministers who believed the Gospel belonged in every hollow and homestead.

As a **blacksmith**, John held one of the community's most essential roles, shaping horseshoes, tools, and wagon parts that kept early Tennessee running. But it was his **spiritual forging** that left the deeper mark. Methodist preachers in that era were known for riding horseback between sparsely settled communities, preaching under trees, in cabins, and in barns. If John followed this path, his story stands at the crossroads of labor and light—serving both with his hands and with his soul. It is easy to imagine him working by fire in daylight, then lighting spiritual fires come evening. His move to Stick in Coffee County may well have been part of this mission: planting Methodist roots in newly forming townships and shaping the moral backbone of the Region.

"The fire of the forge prepared the heart for the fire of the Spirit."
— Local Methodist Saying, c.1830s

🪶 Matilda Ashlin (1805–1870)

Born on **March 6, 1805**, in Tennessee, **Matilda** came into a frontier world still raw and untamed. She was the daughter of **William B. Ashlin (or Alphine)** and **Dicey White**, names echoing through early Southern settlements. Her marriage to **John Adams**, the preacher-blacksmith, around **1818**, made her the spiritual and domestic backbone of a family destined to branch across Coffee County and beyond.

Matilda lived through war scares, religious awakenings, and westward expansion. Though quieter in historical records than her husband, her legacy is deeply felt—in the homes she kept the faith she nurtured, and the generations she carried forward.

She died on **October 26, 1870**, in Tennessee—just after the Civil War had left its mark on the landscape, she had called home for 65 years.

Children:

❧ Benjamin Harrison Adams Sr *(3rd Great-Grandfather)*

Birth: 4 June 1820 — Viola, Warren County, Tennessee **Death:** 9 December 1898 — Stick, Coffee County, Tennessee **Burial:** Manchester, Coffee County, Tennessee

Born just after the War of 1812, Benjamin Harrison Adams Sr. was shaped by frontier grit, Appalachian faith, and the swelling pulse of westward expansion. Son of **John Adams** and **Matilda Ashlin**, he carved out a life as a **blacksmith**, forging not just tools but a legacy that anchored generations.

Benjamin's hands worked iron, but his heart shepherded kin. He appears in every census from **1840 to 1880**, often listed with his occupation proudly marked: *Blacksmith*. His home—be it Hillsboro, Stick, or Manchester—served as a hearth of generational gathering, where children learned trade, scripture, and tenacity. Upon his death in 1898, he left behind a family that stretched like Tennessee ridgelines— sturdy, weathered, and rooted in faith.

James W. Adams *(3rd Great-Granduncle)*

Birth: ~1821 — Tennessee, USA **Death:** 1900 — Tennessee, USA

The second-born son of **John Adams** and **Matilda Ashlin**, James W. entered life when Tennessee was still a newly minted state navigating westward expansion and agrarian promise. By the time his younger brother **Benjamin Harrison Adams Sr.** was born in 1820, the Adams family had settled around Warren and Coffee counties, laying down generational roots that would endure into the next century.

Though his personal life—marriage, children, and profession—remains hazy, James lived through seismic moments: the Civil War, Reconstruction, and Coffee County's emergence as a site of railroads and revived farmland. He outlived both his parents and most siblings, passing away in 1900 at age 79, just two years after his brother Benjamin Sr. died in Stick.

It is likely he was buried in Tennessee soil close to kin, his memory quietly tucked into church records or cemetery ledgers waiting to be named.

Mary Ann Adams *(3rd Great-Grandaunt)*

Birth: 25 October 1829 — Warren County, Tennessee **Death:** 14 August 1895 — Warren County, Tennessee

Though records do not yet confirm her marriage or children, Mary Ann's role within your manuscript feels like a steady keeper of tradition and a guiding hand for younger siblings and local kin. She outlived both parents and remained in Warren County until her passing at age 65.

The simplicity and dignity of her life reflect the quiet strength of so many 19th-century Southern women—unrecorded in headlines, but deeply rooted in the rhythms of hearth, hymn, and harvest.

☽ Sarah E. Adams *(3rd Great-Grandaunt)*

Birth: 19 April 1833 — Coffee County, Tennessee **Death:** 21 April 1903 — Likely Coffee County, Tennessee

She outlived all but a few of her siblings and passed at age 70, just five years after her brother **Benjamin Harrison Adams Sr.**, and within months of her half-brother **Franklin P. White**. Her name appears in family trees and census traces, though her personal story—marriage, children, residence—remains softly veiled.

Her quiet longevity marks her as one of the last matriarchal threads in the Adams family's early fabric. Even without a bold paper trail, her presence helped hold the family canopy together during some of its most transformative years.

🌿 Martha Adams *(3rd Great-Grandaunt)*

Birth: ~1836 — Tennessee, USA **Death:** Unknown

Martha lived through:

- The rise of abolitionist movements and religious revivals in Tennessee
- The Civil War and the transformation of Coffee County's communities
- The passing of all her siblings between 1860 and 1906

Though her marital status and later years remain unrecorded, Martha's timeline places her firmly within the first Adams generation to be born and raised in Tennessee soil. It is possible she lived alongside the family until old age, quietly present in census shadows or unnamed photographs.

🪓 Terumasa Adams *(3rd Great-Granduncle)*

Birth: ~1840 — Coffee County, Tennessee **Death:** Unknown

Notable moments in his timeline include: The death of his father **John Adams** around 1860

- The loss of half-brother **James Buford White** during the Civil War in 1862
- His mother **Matilda's** passing in 1870
- The steady departure of siblings from 1895 through 1906

Though no marriage or death records have been confirmed, it is

Terumasa remained near family—a quiet presence in Hillsboro, Stick, or Monteagle—living past the turn of the century and leaving behind traces yet to be uncovered.

"Faith. Forge. Family."

*A Note to Readers

* Final Thoughts on this Family Tree

*To Future Researchers and Relatives

This history of the Brown and Adams families represent the most accurate and complete. information I had at the time of writing. Every effort has been made to ensure the names,

dates, and relationships are correct based on available records, oral histories, and documentation.

That said, like all family history, this is a living, evolving work. New discoveries may

arise, details may shift, and the story may deepen as more information is uncovered.

This book is not meant to be the final word — it is a foundation. A beginning. A tribute to

those who came before us, and a gift to those who will continue exploring and preserving.

our shared heritage.

In that spirit, I welcome future additions, corrections, and contributions. Our family story is. never truly finished — and that is what makes it so meaningful.

INDEX

Aberdeen, 83, 85

Aberdeen City, 186, 84

ABSOLAM

Absolom, 96, 97

Absolom Billiat, 96, 110, 186

Absolom Billiat, 96, 186

ADAMS

Adams, 142, 1, 4, 5, 11, 12, 15, 27, 136, 138, 139, 140, 142, 143, 144, 145, 146, 149,

Adams A, 7

Adams Anderson, 139, 195

Adams Blair, 162, 199

Adams Born, 151, 157, 199, 201.

Adams Coffee, 173, 205

Adams Eaton, 154, 162, 212

Adams Family, 137, 139, 138, 186

Adams Jr, 172, 189, 155, 157, 159, 160, 161, 162, 163, 166, 167

Adams Line, 136, 186

Adams Rhea, 162, 194

Adams Robert, 15

Adams Siblings, 5, 186

Adams Sr, 165, 176, 179, 189, 202, 206, 5, 160, 165, 166, 167, 168, 180, 182, 177

Adams Warren, 158, 203

ADELPHA

Adelpha, 173

Adelpha Ann, 173, 186

AILEEN

Aileen Brown, 43, 200

AKRON

Akron, 161

ALABAMA

Alabama, 44, 75, 80, 92

Alabama Burial, 186

ALBERT

Albert Warren, 159, 186

ALECK

Aleck, 74, 196

ALENE

Alene Brown, 186

ALEXANDER

Alexander, 65, 66, 67, 69, 70, 71, 72, 73, 77, 78, 79, 80, 81, 87, 91, 96, 100, 101,

Alexander Anderson, 84, 186

Alexander Broun, 124, 128, 129, 130, 133, 134, 186, 193, 130

Alexander Brown, 67, 72, 73, 75, 76, 78, 80, 105, 107, 122, 186, 196, 200, 205

Alexander County, 186, 55

Alexander William, 4, 13, 14, 46, 64, 65, 66, 67, 68, 69, 70, 71, 72, 73, 75, 76,

ALFRED

Alfred Brown, 74, 195

Alfred Henry, 141, 157, 164, 187

ALICE

Alice Brown, 112, 115, 187

ALISON

Alison, 173

Alison Woodville, 166, 167, 172

ALLAN

Allan, 84, 196

ALMA

Alma Jean, 141, 146, 151, 153, 154, 188, 5, 154, 146

ALEXANDER

Alexander William, 82, 188

AMANDA

Amanda, 37, 55

Amanda Brown, 37, 188

AMBROSE

Ambrose Brown, 22, 30, 40, 209

Ambrose Jr, 209, 15

AMERICA

America, 85, 123, 124, 125, 130, 190

America Alexander, 130

America Life, 129

AMERICAN

American Revolution, 120, 93, 119, 121

ANCESTOR

Ancestor Profile, 188

Ancestor ProEiles, 4, 188

ANDERS

Anders Hart, 188, 6

ANDERSON

Anderson, 1, 3, 7, 9, 12, 13, 15, 65, 83, 84, 85, 86, 87, 88, 89, 90, 91, 106, 107,

Anderson A, 2

Anderson Beginning, 139

Anderson Brothers, 17

Anderson Brown, 11

Anderson County, 188, 96, 99

Anderson I, 11

Anderson Sr, 205, 140

ANDREW

Andrew, 42, 46, 55, 160, 161, 211

Andrew Brown, 42, 195, 211

Andrew Campbell, 60, 209

Andrew Lawrence, 141, 160, 188, 145, 157

ANN

Ann Adams, 166, 167, 173, 181, 186, 201

Ann Brown, 25, 30, 40, 60, 98, 99, 117, 198, 205, 206

Ann Meniza, 101, 105, 113, 116, 194

Ann Nobles, 151, 205

ANNA

Anna, 110, 111

Anna Ash, 93, 110, 112, 113, 114, 115, 116, 188

ANNIE

Annie E, 39

Annie Margaret, 188

ANSON

Anson County, 109, 188, 109, 118, 122, 123, 126 APPALACHIAN

Appalachian, 49, 50, 51, 57, 59, 60, 63, 69, 73, 77, 82, 111, 116, 130, 176, 180

ARCHIBALD

Archibald, 105, 107, 108, 209

Archibald Brown, 4, 14, 82, 92, 93, 94, 96, 97, 99, 100, 101, 102, 103, 104, 105,

ARKANSAS

Arkansas Burial, 188

ARMSTRONG

Armstrong Cemetery, 27, 188

ARMY

Army, 92

ASHLIN

Ashlin, 165, 177, 179, 180, 201

AUBREY

Aubrey, 144, 188

Aubrey L, 143

Aubrey Lee, 142, 5, 12, 15, 27, 139, 141, 142, 146, 151, 152, 188
Aubrey Married, 15

AUDY

Audy, 21, 22

Audy Iowa, 20, 21, 29, 189, 15

AUGUSTA

Augusta County, 120, 189, 93, 119, 121, 123

AUSTIN

Austin, 46, 65, 66, 67, 68, 69, 70, 71, 72, 73, 75, 76, 77, 79, 80, 81, 87

BALDWIN

Baldwin Henderson, 38, 211

BANFF

Banff, 125

BARBARA

Barbara, 129

Barbara Randell, 124, 129, 189

BARHAM

Barham, 101, 102, 201

BATTLEFIELD

Battlefield, 75

BENJAMIN

Benjamin, 67, 70, 79, 87, 156, 165, 167, 194

Benjamin Brown, 69, 72, 75, 80, 194

Benjamin Harrison, 5, 145, 155, 157, 159, 160, 161, 162, 163, 165, 167, 168,

Benjamin Jr, 189, 168, 172, 173, 174

Benjamin Sr, 189, 165, 181

BERNICE

Bernice Brown, 189

BERTHA

Bertha May, 189

Bertha Zumbro, 161, 189

BESSIE

Bessie, 15, 25, 27, 194

Bessie Mae, 3, 4, 8, 12, 14, 16, 17, 18, 19, 28, 29, 139, 143, 189, 210

BETHEL

Bethel Church, 120, 189, 119

BILES

Biles, 9

BILL

Bill, 57, 211

Bill Brown, 189

BILLIAT

Billiat, 11

Billiat Brown, 96, 186

BILLOAT

Billiat Brown, 96, 186

BLACK

Black, 93, 118, 122, 126, 191

BLACKSMITH

Blacksmith, 165, 180

BLAIR

Blair, 162, 199, 212

BLESSING

BLUE

Blue Ribbon, 204, 25

Blue Ridge, 189, 110

BOB

Bob Sherwood, 189, 9, 10

BON

Bon Air, 189

BOONE

Boone Counties, 68

Boone

BOYD

Boyd, 4, 41, 198, 203

Boyd Nola, 34

Boyd Second, 34

BRIAN

Brian Keith, 1, 2, 3, 7, 11, 16, 17, 190

BROTHERS

Brothers, 17

BROUN

Broun, 124, 128, 129, 130, 133, 134, 186, 193, 197

Broun Shield, 128

BROWN

Brown, 4, 10, 12, 13, 14, 15, 17, 18, 20, 21, 24, 25, 28, 29, 30, 34, 35, 36, 37, 38,

Brown Barham, 101, 201

Brown Birth, 18, 19, 20, 25, 26, 64, 187, 189, 190, 195, 206

Brown Born, 12

Brown Campbell, 60, 198

Brown Chapter, 133

Brown Family, 4, 11, 17, 27

Brown Full, 64

Brown Henderson, 37, 199

Brown I, 117

Brown I, 93, 118, 119, 120, 121, 122, 123, 124, 125, 129, 130, 133,

130

Brown Iii, 117, 125, 134

Brown Isabel, 84

Brown Jr, 209, 211, 22, 30, 40, 48

Brown May 3, 189

Brown Nickname, 197 Buren County 34, 210

BURLINGTON

Burlington County, 112

BURR

Burr Riddle, 41, 42, 199, 211

BYRNE

Byrne, 101, 103, 104, 105, 110, 117, 191, 206

Byrne Brown, 108, 111, 112, 114, 115, 116, 206

CAMPBELL

Campbell, 60, 198, 209

Campbell County, 120, 121, 122

CANADA

Canada, 121

Canada Brown, 118, 119, 120, 121, 192

CARD

Card Boyd, 4, 34, 41, 203

CAROLIN

Carolin Despite, 126

CAROLINA

Carolina, 93, 94, 97, 98, 99, 100, 101, 103, 104, 105, 109, 110, 113, 118, 120,

Carolina Died, 207

CAROLINAS

Carolinas, 104, 111

CAROLINE

Caroline, 48, 49, 50, 51, 53, 59, 70, 71, 73, 77, 78, 79, 80, 81, 87

Caroline Brown, 52, 77, 89

CAROLINIAN

Carolinian, 98

CARROLL

Carroll Fults, 56, 197

CARTER

Carter Brown, 88

CATHERINE

Catherine Black, 93, 118, 122, 126, 191

CELIA

Celia, 108

Celia Green, 82, 93, 94, 96, 97, 99, 100, 101, 102, 103, 104, 105, 106, 108, 109,

CENSUS

Census, 49, 65, 66, 71, 84, 85, 87, 88, 93, 146, 159, 162, 170, 175, 192

CENSUSES

Censuses, 107, 192

CENTURY

Century Edinburgh, 129

CHAPEL

Chapel, 146, 211

Chapel Cemetery, 211, 10

CHAPTER

Chapter From, 133

CHARLES

Charles, 172

Charles Alison, 172, 173

Charles Creek, 29

CHARLOTTA

Charlotta, 86

CHESTER

Chester, 195

Chester Brown, 20, 29, 40, 195

CHESTINE

Chestine Adams, 160

CHILDREN

Children, 13, 209

Children Josephine, 36

CHRISTAN

Christan Keer, 125

CHRISTIAN

Christian Coop, 60

CHRONICLE

Chronicle, 2, 7

CHURCH

Church, 120, 189

CINDY

Cindy Lynn, 9

Civil District, 44, 146, 170, 173

Civil Districts, 56, 190

Civil War, 66, 67, 71, 72, 75, 77, 92, 169, 179, 182, 183, 190, 209, 47, 54, 70, 87, 91,

97, 98, 108, 114, 170, 181, 114

CLARA

Clara, 18

Clara Ellen, 18, 29, 190, 15

CLAY

Clay County, 190, 66

CLEMENTS

Clements, 85

CLEVELAND

Cleveland Adams, 170, 194

COFFEE

Coffee, 30, 39, 65, 75, 151, 166, 167, 170, 180

Coffee Counties, 66, 71, 73, 177

Coffee County, 12, 41, 42, 43, 44, 46, 55, 56, 60, 61, 140, 154, 165, 169, 171, 12, 15,

19, 25, 26, 28, 29, 42, 139, 142, 145, 151, 152, 153, 154, 152, 161, 169

Coffee County's, 45

COLLEGE

College Cemetery, 196, 26

COLONIAL

Colonial America, 123, 124, 125, 129, 130, 190, 130

Colonial Maryland, 117, 118, 126, 190

COMMERCE

Commerce Street, 85, 190

COMMUNITY

Community, 191

CONFEDERATE

Confederate, 75

CONWAY

Conway County, 51, 190

CORNELIA

Cornelia, 48, 49, 50

Cornelia A, 49

County Down, 122, 190, 122

County Married, 12, 13

COVE

Cove, 56, 193

CREEK

Creek, 202

Creek Cemetery, 86, 191, 86

CROSSLAND

Crossland Adams, 167, 203

CUMBERLAND

Cumberland Plateau, 190, 54

CURTIS

Curtis, 83, 86, 88, 89, 90, 91

Curtis Brown, 88

CUYAHOGA

Cuyahoga County, 191, 142, 143, 152, 152

DAISY

Daisy Lynn, 191, 9

DALLAS

Dallas County, 191, 23

DASSIE

Dassie Rogers, 191

Dassie Tate, 43, 191

DAVID

David Brown, 109, 191

David Harris, 191

David McCarter, 86, 90

David T, 56

DAVIDSON

Davidson County, 43, 52, 94, 191, 94, 139, 154, 155

DAYLIGHT

Daylight, 91

Daylight Community, 191, 18

DEDICATION

Dedication, 4

DEEP

Deep South, 191, 66

DELPHA

Delpha, 186

DENNIS

Dennis, 153

DEPOT

Depot Bottom, 57, 63, 58

DEPRESSION

Depression, 30, 194

DESCENDANT

Descendant Highlights, 4, 191

DIANE

Diane Eaton, 155, 204

DICEY

Dicey White, 179, 191 DICKESON

Dickeson, 129, 200

DICKIE

Dickie Dickeson, 200

DILLARD

Dillard Roy, 191

DOAK

Doak, 119, 120, 197, 202

Doak Brown, 118, 121, 197

DOTARD

Dotard Brown, 191

DRUCILLA

Drucilla Knight, 208, 29

DUNN

Dunn Creek, 86, 191

DUTCH

Dutch Brown, 45, 197

EATON

Eaton, 154, 155, 162, 197, 198, 204, 212

Eaton Wilma, 154

EDINBURGH

Edinburgh, 124, 125, 129, 130, 133, 134

Edinburgh Alexander, 129

Edinburgh Scotland, 132

EDWARD

Edward, 50, 62, 67, 78, 87, 211

Edward Brown, 4, 13, 46, 47, 48, 49, 50, 51, 52, 53, 54, 56, 57, 58, 59, 60, 61,

Edward Jr, 211, 48

ELDEST

Eldest, 168

ELIJAH

Elijah Adams, 177, 191

ELISEBETH

Elisebeth Boyd, 198, 34

ELIZA

Eliza Jane, 92, 191

ELIZABETH

Elizabeth, 48, 49, 50, 52, 59, 60, 67, 69, 70, 72, 77, 79, 80, 82, 83, 86, 87, 89, 91,

Elizabeth Adams, 158, 166, 167, 168, 201, 203

Elizabeth Brown, 37, 44, 51, 70, 74, 75, 89, 90, 107, 113, 191, 197, 199, 202, 205

Elizabeth Byrne, 191

Elizabeth Byrne -Buckner -Brown, 118

Elizabeth Catherine, 93, 118, 122, 126, 191

Elizabeth Crossland, 141, 166, 167, 168, 202, 203

Elizabeth Wooten, 169, 202

ELLEN

Ellen, 190

Ellen Brown, 18, 29, 40, 190

ELLICT

Ellict Andrew, 60, 209

ELSEY

Elsey Winton, 9

ELVIRA

Elvira, 70, 71, 73, 75, 76, 77, 87

Elvira Brown, 75, 192

Elvira Matida, 157

ELVOWERY

Elvowery, 60

EMALINE

Emaline, 48, 54, 56, 57, 59, 62, 202

Emaline Williams, 46, 47, 49, 50, 51, 52, 53, 54, 56, 57, 58, 59, 60, 61, 63, 68,

EMILINE

Emiline, 60, 210

EMMA

Emma, 74, 200

EMMALINE

Emmaline Rogers, 44, 202

ERWIN

Erwin, 89

EUCLY

Eucly, 193

Eucly Adams, 159, 193

EWLEOH

Ewloe, 26

FAMILIES

Families Zumbro, 196, 5

FAMILY

Family Faith, 137

Family Legacy, 17, 27

Family Line, 139, 138, 186

Family Lineage, 4, 11

Family Tree, 184, 192

FANNIE

Fannie, 50

FATE

Fate Lynn, 192, 9

FAUQUIER

Fauquier County, 111, 192, 110, 114, 115

FEDERAL

Federal Census, 175, 192

Federal Censuses, 107, 192

FELIX

Felix, 120, 121

Felix Canada, 119, 120, 121, 192

Final Thoughts, 184, 192

First Brown, 130, 192

FLOYD

Floyd Counties, 77, 78

FOSTER

Foster Price, 192

FRANCE

France, 60, 199

FRANCES

Frances, 96, 100, 101, 103, 104, 105, 107, 108, 110, 112, 114

Frances Hobbs, 63, 201

Frances Riddle, 42, 203

Frances Sanders, 74, 198

FRANCIS

Francis Brown, 63, 200

FRANK

Frank, 13, 55

Frank Brown, 192, 9

Frank Stroud, 192

FRANKIE

Frankie, 108

FRANKLIN

Franklin County, 192, 157

Franklin P, 182

FREDONIA

Fredonia, 153

FRENCH

French, 119, 120

FRONIE

Fronie, 72, 73, 78, 81, 201L

FULTON

Fulton County, 193, 88

FULTS

Fults, 56, 197

Fults Cove, 56, 193

GENERATION

Generation Overview, 4

GEORGE

George, 96, 100, 101, 103, 110, 112, 159, 198

George Ash, 110, 193

George Brown, 103, 193

George County, 198, 118

George Eucly, 141, 159, 193, 145, 157

George I, 118

George Lynn, 193, 9

George M, 125

George Morrison, 125, 193

GEORGIA

Georgia, 48, 66

GERMAN

German, 21

GIBERT

Gibert Henderson, 38

GILBERT

Gilbert Rogers, 193

GILLEY

Gilley Lynn, 193, 9

GILLIE

Gillie B, 51

GLADYS

Gladys, 153

Gladys Marie, 151, 152, 194, 146

Gladys Riddle, 42, 194

GLASGOW

Glasgow, 129

Grace Gladys, 194

GRANDAUNT

Grandaunt Parents, 194

GRANDFATHER

Grandfather Parents, 194

Grandfather Spouse, 194

Grandfather William, 141, 194

GRANDMOTHER

Grandmother Parents, 194

Grandmother Spouse, 194

GRANDUNCLE

Granduncle Born, 69

Granduncle Parents, 194

GRANNIE

Grannie, 25, 26, 147

Grannie Bessie, 25, 194

Great Awakening, 103, 207

Great Depression, 30, 194, 153, 162, 172

GREEK

Greek, 174

GREEN

Green, 82, 93, 94, 96, 97, 99, 100, 101, 102, 103, 104, 105, 106, 108, 109, 112,

GREENBERRY

Greenberry, 69, 77, 78, 81

Greenberry Austin, 66

Greenberry Benjamin, 67, 69, 70, 79, 87, 194

Greenberry Jane, 81

GREENOCK

Greenock, 129

GROGAN

Grogan, 66, 206

GROVE

Grove, 42, 207

GROVER

Grover, 170

Grover Clevelan

GRUNDY

Grundy, 48, 59, 61, 63, 75

Grundy Counties, 167, 49, 170, 166

Grundy County, 37, 46, 51, 55, 56, 60, 81, 82, 96, 153, 167, 168, 194, 196, 25, 27, 39,

44, 47, 49, 56, 57, 60, 73, 78, 94, 143, 152, 156, 167, 168

HAMILTON

Hamilton County, 48, 194

HAMPDEN

Hampden County, 194, 124

HANNAH

Hannah Ann, 101, 105, 113, 116, 194

HARDIN

Hardin Counties, 75

Hardin County, 195, 75

HARMON

Harmon, 20

Harmon Chester, 20, 29, 195, 15

HARRIS

Harris Brown, 39, 191

HARRISON

Harrison, 60, 206

Harrison Aams, 145

Harrison Adams, 5, 155, 157, 159, 160, 161, 162, 163, 165, 166, 167, 168, 172,

Harrison Blair, 162, 212

Harrison County, 195, 69

HART

Hart, 188

HARVEY

Harvey D, 92

HAZEL

Hazel Irene, 195

HELEN

Helen, 140, 144

Helen Cry, 195

Helen Maxine, 4, 8, 11, 12, 15, 27, 139, 140, 142, 143, 144, 195

HOBBS

Hobbs, 63, 201

HOLLOW

Hollow, 40, 41, 55, 205

HORTON

Horton, 51, 199

HOSTON

Hoston Brown, 209

HOUSTON

Houston Brown, 4, 12, 15, 18, 28, 29, 34, 40, 47, 209

Houston Lynn, 195, 9

Houston Sr, 209, 13

IASSC

Issac Andrew, 19

ILLINOIS

Illinois, 55, 92

IMOGENE

Imogene, 27

INDIAN

Indian War, 120, 196, 119

INDIANA

Indiana, 20, 22, 23

Indiana Thomas, 22

Industrial Revolution, 85

INTERTWINED

Intertwined Families, 5, 196

INTRODUCTION

Introduction, 4

IOLA

Iola Henderson, 38, 205

IOWA

Iowa, 189

Iowa Brown, 20, 21, 29, 40, 189

IRELAND

Ireland, 122, 203

Ireland Died, 203

IRENE

Irene Adams, 160, 195

IRISH

Irish, 110, 120, 123

IRVING

Irving College, 26, 196, 27

ISAAC

Isaac, 30, 38, 40, 43, 47, 50, 51, 52, 53, 54, 55, 58, 60, 74, 75, 76, 81, 83, 90, 91,

Isaac Alexander, 67, 69, 70, 71, 73, 77, 78, 79, 87, 196

Isaac Anderson, 86, 196

Isaac B, 4, 12, 36, 37, 38, 39, 40, 41, 42, 44, 45, 46, 48, 54, 56, 69, 13

Isaac Brown, 23, 35, 88, 89, 196, 197

Isaac Henderson, 38, 205

ISABEL

Isabel, 85

Isabel Anderson, 83, 84, 107, 196

ISABELLA

Isabella, 85

Isabella Brown, 85, 196

ISOBEL

Isobel, 85

Isobel Allan, 84, 196

IVA

Iva Adams, 196

IZARD

Izard County, 92, 196, 88, 91, 92

JACKSON

Jackson County, 196, 88

JACOB

Jacob, 49, 50, 51, 56

Jacob B, 48, 50, 68

JAMES

James, 48, 50, 52, 53, 54, 58, 66, 71, 73, 77, 78, 80, 86, 87, 181

James Aleck, 74, 196

James Broun, 128, 129

James Brown, 53, 197

James Randolph, 42, 197

James W, 180, 177

James Wendell, 154, 197

JANE

Jane, 48, 50, 52, 53, 54, 56, 58, 59, 60, 61, 71, 73, 77, 78, 80, 81, 87, 120, 175,

Jane Adams, 166, 167, 171, 174, 197, 206

Jane Brown, 55, 56, 68, 74, 79, 197, 206

Jane McNew, 157

Jane Mitchell, 118, 119, 120, 121, 197

Jane Narmore, 92, 191

JAY

Jay F, 56

JEAN

Jean, 146, 151, 154, 188, 212

Jean Adams, 153, 154, 162, 188, 212

JEESE

Jeese Thurman, 12, 15, 27, 141, 197

JEFFERSON

Jefferson, 51

Jefferson County, 197, 92

JENNIE

Jennie M, 159

JERSEY

Jersey, 99, 111, 112, 203

Jersey Died, 203

JESSE

Jesse Lee, 197, 151

JESSIE

Jessie, 153

JEWELL

Jewell Dutch, 45, 197

Jewell Elizabeth, 197

JOHN

John, 62, 63, 66, 68, 71, 73, 76, 77, 80, 86, 87, 89, 90, 92, 102, 170, 177, 178,

John A, 74

John Adams, 165, 177, 178, 179, 180, 183, 197

John B, 92

John Brown, 76, 83, 91, 197

John Buckner, 96, 100, 102, 104, 108, 110, 112, 114, 197

John Bud, 46, 48, 51, 53, 54, 55, 56, 58, 59, 61, 62, 63, 197

John Carroll, 56, 197

John Isaac, 23, 30, 197

John McCarter, 86, 90

John R, 29

John Wesley, 169, 198

John William, 151, 198

JOHNNIE

Johnnie, 24, 153

Johnnie B, 151, 153, 146

Johnnie Brown, 198

JOHNSON

Johnson County, 92, 198

JOSEPH

Joseph, 50, 86, 90

JOSEPHINE

Josephine, 36, 37, 43, 45, 55

Josephine Frances, 74, 198

Josephine Hill, 36, 198

JUEL

Juel Brown, 198

JULY

July 28, 37, 40, 48, 49, 64, 65, 69, 87, 88, 89, 90, 119, 159, 163, 169, 175

JUNE

June 3, 15, 19, 23, 26, 28, 29, 41, 44, 45, 47, 48, 56, 61, 63, 68, 73, 73, 74, 78, 80,

KEER

Keer, 125

KEITH

Keith Anderson, 1, 2, 3, 7, 9, 11, 16, 17, 190

KENNETH

Kenneth Anderson, 139, 140, 205

Kenneth Eaton, 198

KENTUCKY

Kentucky, 69, 80, 84

Kentucky Burial, 20, 198

KING

King George, 118, 198

KNIGHT

Knight, 208

KNOTT

Knott, 5, 145, 157, 158, 159, 160, 161, 162, 163, 164, 165

Knott Adams, 157

KNOX

Knox County, 94, 198

LAMAR

Lamar County, 169, 198, 169

LAURA

Laura, 81, 89

Laura A, 73, 78, 80, 81, 87

Laura Ann, 48, 53, 54, 59, 60, 61, 62, 198, 58

LAVINA

Lavina Elisebeth, 34, 198

LAWRENCE

Lawrence, 188

Lawrence Adams, 160, 188

Lawrence County, 198, 99

Lawrence Greenberry, 66, 198

LEE

Lee Adams, 142, 5, 12, 15, 27, 139, 142, 146, 152, 160, 162, 189, 206

Lee Brown, 26, 30, 41, 198

LEGACY

Legacy Born, 118

Legacy Elizabeth, 122

Legacy Helen, 125

Legacy Jane, 120

Legacy Note, 8, 199

Legacy Notes, 4, 199

Legacy Title, 199

Legacy William, 124

LENA

Lena, 162

Lena Horton, 51, 199

Lena May, 162, 199, 145, 157

LETA

Leta, 151

Leta Neva, 5, 141, 142, 146, 151, 154, 161, 199

LEVI

Levi France, 60, 199

LEWIS

Lewis County, 90, 199, 90

LIFE

Life, 118, 120, 122, 124, 125, 129

LIKELY

Likely, 14, 169, 171

Coffee, 172, 182

Henderson, 171

Virginia, 94

LILLIE

Lillie M, 42

Lillie Mae, 199

LINCOLN

Lincoln County, 55, 199, 28, 40, 177

LINE

Line, 4, 14, 136, 186, 209

Line Robert, 139

Line The, 138

LINEAGE

Lineage Timeline, 4, 11

LIVING

Living, 171

LIZZIE

Lizzie, 38, 55

Lizzie Rosie, 37, 43, 45, 199, 13

LLOYD

Lloyd Randall, 199

LOCAL

Local Methodist, 179, 199

LOU

Lou Rogers, 36, 192

LOUIS

Louis, 66, 67, 78

Louis Alexander, 67, 70, 77, 78, 79, 80, 81, 87, 199

LOUISA

Louisa, 48, 53, 54, 58, 59, 62, 86

Louisa Brown, 59, 200

LOUISE

Louise Brown, 39, 188

LOUISIANA

Louisiana Burial, 200

LOUVENIA

Louvenia, 60

LOWER

Lower Potomack, 117, 118, 124, 125, 126, 200

LUCINDA

Lucinda, 37, 38, 41, 42, 43, 45, 55, 201

Lucinda Brown, 41, 201

LUCRETIA

Lucretia, 60

LUHANY

Luh any, 86

LYDIA

Lydia, 115

Lydia Brown, 114, 116, 200

LYNN

Lynn, 12, 35, 36, 37, 38, 39, 40, 41, 42, 44, 45, 55, 191, 192, 193, 195, 200

Mack

Mack Brown, 200

MACK

Mack, 37, 39, 43, 45, 46, 205, 206

Mack Brown, 39, 206

MADISON

Madison County, 170, 196, 200, 92, 170

MAE

Mae Brown, 19

Mae Brown, 3, 4, 12, 14, 17, 18, 19, 28, 29, 40, 143, 189, 210, 8, 139, 16

Mae Riddle, 42, 199

MAGGIE

Maggie, 43

Maggie Lynn, 35

Maggie Margaret, 12, 36, 37, 38, 39, 40, 41, 42, 44, 45, 55, 200

MANCHESTER

Manchester, 61, 153, 172, 174

MARCENA

Marcena, 92

MARCUS

Marcus, 50

MARGARET

Margaret, 29, 96, 97, 110, 128

Margaret Brown, 97, 200, 18

Margaret Dickie, 200

Margaret Emma, 74, 200

Margaret Louise, 39, 188

Margaret Lynn, 12, 36, 37, 38, 39, 40, 41, 42, 44, 45, 55, 200

Margaret Mary, 110, 117, 200

Margaret Susan, 4, 12, 15, 18, 28, 29, 40, 200

Margaret Susie, 141, 200

MARGIE

Margie Aileen, 200

MARIE

Marie, 151, 194

Marie Adams, 152, 162, 194

MARION

Marion County, 160, 200

Marion Francis, 63, 200

MARJORIE

Marjorie Brown, 200

MARRIAGE

Marriage, 54

MARRIED

Married, 12, 15, 140.

Married Maggie, 12, 200

Married Margaret, 12, 200

Married Nancy, 13, 200

Married Rachel, 13

MARSENA

Marsena F, 92

MARSHALL

Marshall, 74, 211

MARTHA

Martha, 48, 53, 54, 59, 60, 101, 169, 182, 212 Martha Adams, 169, 182, 201

Martha Brown, 58, 201

Martha Lucinda, 37, 38, 41, 42, 43, 45, 55, 201

Martha Matilda, 177

Martha Patty, 97, 100, 101, 110, 112

MARY

Mary, 81, 110, 117, 157, 176, 200

Mary A, 56

Mary Ann, 181, 201, 177

Mary Elizabeth, 168, 201

Mary Frances, 63, 201

Mary Fronie, 81, 201

Mary Knott, 164

Mary Narcissa, 74, 201

Mary Sophronia, 67, 69, 70, 72, 73, 77, 80, 87, 201

Mary Winston, 5, 145, 157, 158, 159, 160, 161, 162, 163, 201

Mary Winton, 141, 158, 201

MARYLAND

Maryland, 118, 124, 125, 190

Maryland Died, 190

MASSACHUSETTS

Massachusetts, 124, 125, 126, 130

MATIDA

Matida Jane, 157

MATILDA

Matilda, 86, 179

Matilda Ashlin, 165, 177, 179, 180

MATRIARCH

Matriarch, 17, 209

MATTISON

Mattison Monroe, 173, 174, 176

MAXINE

Maxine, 142

Maxine Adams, 4, 11, 12, 15, 27, 139, 144, 195, 8, 139

MAY

May Adams, 162, 199

MCBRAYNE

McBrayne Brown, 93, 117, 118, 119, 120, 121, 122, 123, 124, 125, 129, 130,

MCCARTER

McCarter, 86, 90

MCCRACKEN

McCracken County, 20

MCMAHON

McMahon, 12, 27

McMahon Jeese, 15

MCMINNVILLE

McMinnville, 27, 46, 48, 55, 60, 63, 77

MELISSA

Melissa Elizabeth, 169, 202

MENIZA

Meniza, 101, 105, 113, 194

Meniza Brown, 116, 194

METHODIST

Methodist, 178, 179

Methodist Saying, 199, 179

MICHIGAN

Michigan City, 202, 22

MIDDLE

Middle Tennessee, 202, 165, 155, 167

MIDWESTERN

Midwestern, 113, 143

MILTON

Milton, 37

Milton Rogers, 36, 202

MINERVA

Minerva Henderson, 38, 212

MINNIE

Minnie, 45

Minnie Waldean, 202

MITCHELL

Mitchell Doak, 118, 119, 120, 121, 197, 202

MONONGALIA

Monongalia County, 114, 202, 113, 115, 116, 114

MONROE

Monroe, 173, 201

Monroe Adams, 166, 168, 174, 176, 202

Monroe County, 133, 202, 117, 118, 119, 120, 121, 126, 134

MONTEAGLE

Monteagle, 174

MORGAN

Morgan County, 202, 44

MORRISON

Morrison, 117, 124, 125, 193, 195

MOTHER

Mother Emaline, 54, 59, 62, 202

Mother Rachel, 80, 202

MOUNT

Mount Zion, 63, 202

MOUNTAIN

Mountain Creek, 202, 177, 178

MYRTLE

Myrtle, 45

Myrtle Emmaline, 44, 202

NANCY

Nancy, 76, 78, 86, 96, 108, 110, 114, 167, 174

Nancy Anderson, 13, 65, 83, 85, 86, 87, 88, 89, 90, 91, 106, 107, 200, 202

Nancy Brown, 100, 202

Nancy Elizabeth, 67, 69, 70, 72, 77, 79, 80, 82, 83, 87, 89, 90, 91, 141, 166, 167, 168,

202

Nancy J, 74

NAPOLEONIC

Napoleonic Wars, 203, 85

NARCISSA

Narcissa Brown, 74, 201

NARMORE

Narmore Thompson, 92, 191

NASHVILLE

Nashville, 43, 154, 155

NELL

Nell Frances, 203

NEVA

Neva Zumbro, 5, 146, 151, 154, 161, 199, 142

NEW

New Jersey, 99, 111, 112, 203

New Orleans, 203, 163

New York, 203, 159

NEWTON

Newton County, 203, 88, 89

NICHOLAS

Nicholas, 85

NOBLES

Nobles, 151, 205

NOLA

Nola, 34

Nola Card, 4, 34, 41, 203

NORA

Nora, 159, 173

Nora Elizabeth, 158, 203

NORTH

North, 109

North Carolin, 126

North Carolina, 94, 97, 98, 99, 100, 101, 103, 104, 105, 109, 110, 113, 118, 120, 121,

123, 124, 94, 100, 101, 105, 109, 121, 122, 177, 178, 97

NORTHERN

Northern Ireland, 122, 203

OHIO

Ohio, 103, 113, 143, 162, 196

Ohio Aubrey, 142, 152

Ohio Burial, 203

OKLAHOMA

Oklahoma, 49

OLD

Old World, 110, 125, 126, 203

PEARL

Pearl Rogers, 36, 203

PEARSON

Pearson, 210

Pearson Adams, 163, 210

PEDEN

Peden, 4, 12, 28, 29, 40, 200

Peden Birth, 28, 200

Peden First, 29

PENDLETON

Pendleton, 193

Pendleton District, 96, 99, 204

PHILADELPHIA

Philadelphia, 74

PHILLIPS

Phillips, 5

PIKE

Pike County, 204, 20 PINEVILLE

Pineville Cemetery, 92, 204, 91

PLACES

Places Aberdeen, 186

Places Alfred, 141

PONTOTOC

Pontotoc County, 204, 49

PORTE

Porte County, 198, 22

POTOMACK

Potomack Hundred, 118, 200, 117, 124, 125, 126

PREBLE

Preble County, 204, 112, 113

PRESBYTERIAN

Presbyterian, 84, 120, 122, 125, 129

PRESTON

Preston County, 204, 110, 111

PRICE

Price Brown, 39, 192

Price Henderson, 38, 192

PRINCE

Prince William, 102, 111, 113, 114, 115, 116, 204

PUTNAM

Putnam County, 204, 12, 14, 18, 19

RACHEL

Rachel, 66, 70, 72, 77, 80, 81, 202

Rachel Austin, 46, 65, 66, 67, 68, 69, 70, 71, 72, 73, 75, 76, 77, 79, 80, 81, 87

Rachel Elizabeth, 74

Rachel Savannah, 56, 205

RAGSDALE

Ragsdale Road, 152, 205

RANDALL

Randall Brown, 43, 199

RANDELL

Randell, 124, 129, 189

RANDOLPH

Randolph, 42

Randolph Riddle, 42, 197

RAY

Ray Mack, 37, 205

RAYBURN

Rayburn Iola, 205

REBECCA

Rebecca, 99

Rebecca Ann, 96, 98, 99, 108, 110, 114, 151, 205

RECONSTRUCTION

Reconstruction, 75, 91, 169, 174

REED

Reed, 74, 159, 205

REVOLUTION

Revolution, 120

REVOLUTIONARY

Revolutionary, 97, 119, 126

Revolutionary War, 82, 93, 96, 97, 99, 100, 101, 102, 104, 105, 106,

108, 109, 94

RHEA

Rhea, 162, 194

RICHARD

Richard, 70, 71, 79

Richard Alexander, 73, 77, 78, 80, 87, 205

RIDDLE

Riddle, 41, 42, 188, 194, 197, 199, 201, 203, 211

RIDGE

Ridge, 189

ROANE

Roane County, 205, 13, 82, 106

ROARING

Roaring Twenties, 79

ROBERT

Robert, 27, 146, 147, 148, 161, 162, 209

Robert Adams, 146, 205

Robert Bob, 60, 61, 205

Robert E, 15, 26, 30

Robert Isaac, 205

Robert Kenneth, 139, 140, 205

Robert L, 12, 15, 27

Robert Taylor, 5, 141, 142, 145, 151, 154, 159, 160, 161, 162, 163, 168, 173, 205,

157

ROGER

Roger Hollow, 40, 41, 55, 205, 37, 39, 44.

ROGERS

Rogers, 36, 37, 44, 191, 192, 193, 195, 198, 202, 203

ROSIE

Rosie, 37, 43, 45, 199

Rosie Elizabeth, 37, 199

ROWAN

Rowan County, 206, 94, 105

ROY

Roy B, 45, 13

Roy Brown, 9, 206

Roy Harrison, 60, 206

Roy Mack, 39, 43, 45, 206

Roy Rogers, 36, 191

RUFUS

Rufus Lee, 206

RUTH

Ruth, 25

Ruth Ann, 25, 30, 206, 15

SALLIE

Sallie, 71, 77, 82, 87, 206

Sallie Brown, 71, 89, 90, 207

Sallie Jane, 74, 206

SAMUEL

Samuel, 48, 56, 58, 59, 62, 116, 175

Samuel Brown, 61, 206

Samuel Byrne, 101, 103, 104, 105, 108, 114, 115, 116, 206

Samuel Henry, 175, 206

SAN

San Antonio, 206, 30, 41

SANDERS

Sanders, 74, 198

SARAH

Sarah, 13, 70, 72, 78, 101, 105, 112, 116

Sarah A, 67, 69, 70, 72, 76, 87

Sarah Curtis, 86

Sarah E, 181, 177

Sarah Grogan, 66, 206

Sarah Jane, 48, 50, 52, 53, 54, 56, 58, 59, 60, 61, 68, 171, 175, 206

Sarah Sallie, 71, 77, 82, 87, 89, 90, 206

Sarah Wilson, 177, 207

SAVANNAH

Savannah, 56, 205

SCOTLAND

Scotland, 124, 125, 129, 132

Scotland Burial, 207

Scotland Died, 207

SCOTS

Scots, 123, 210

SCOTSMAN

Scotsman, 133

SCOTTISH

Scottish, 83, 85, 130

SEQUATCHIE

Sequatchie County, 108, 109, 207, 107

SEVIER

Sevier Counties, 86

Sevier County, 207, 85, 86, 86

SHADY

Shady Grove, 42, 207

SHENANDOAH

Shenandoah Valley, 207

SHERWOOD

Sherwood, 189

SHIELD

Shield Azure, 128

SHILOH

Shiloh Battlefield, 75

SMITH

Smith, 66

Smith Counties, 65

Smith County, 46, 48, 196, 207, 68

SMOKY

Smoky Mountains, 207, 86

SOPHRONIA

Sophronia, 67, 69, 70, 72, 73, 75, 77, 80, 87, 201

SPIRITUAL

Spiritual Reflections, 5

STONE

Stone County, 92, 207, 71

Stone House, 111, 207, 110

STROUD

Stroud Warren, 159, 192

SUMMIT

Summit, 159

Summit County, 208, 160, 162, 163

SUSAN

Susan, 86

Susan Adams, 166, 168, 175, 208

Susan Drucilla, 29, 208

Susan Peden, 4, 12, 15, 28, 29, 40, 200, 18

SUSIE

Susie Peden, 200

TATE

Tate, 43, 191

TAYLOR

Taylor, 205

Taylor Adams, 5, 142, 145, 149, 151, 154, 159, 160, 161, 162, 163, 168, 169,

TENNESSEE

Tennessee, 2, 17, 18, 19, 25, 28, 34, 36, 37, 38, 39, 40, 41, 42, 43, 44, 45, 46, 47,

Tennessee Born, 29, 180

Tennessee Browns, 123, 208

Tennessee Burial, 25, 26, 29, 208

Tennessee Cause, 93, 208

Tennessee Celia, 94

Tennessee Children, 36

Tennessee Clara, 18

Tennessee Death, 208

Tennessee Died, 208

Tennessee Ewloe, 26

Tennessee Gladys, 152

Tennessee Great, 208

Tennessee Great -Grandfather, 28

Tennessee Harmon, 20

Tennessee His, 145, 176

Tennessee Johnnie, 153

Tennessee Margaret, 28

Tennessee Nola, 34

Tennessee Passed, 139, 142, 145, 208.

Tennessee River, 208, 49

Tennessee She, 139, 174, 182

Tennessee Though, 181

TERUMASA

Terumasa, 183

Terumasa Adams, 177, 183, 208

TEXAS

Texas, 23, 24, 160

Texas Burial, 23, 208

THE

The Adams, 137, 139, 138, 208

The Browns, 46, 69, 89

The Carolina, 177, 209

The Civil, 209

The Gathering, 209

The Line, 4, 14, 209

The Matriarch, 17, 209

The Pictures, 10, 209

The Unboxed, 1, 2, 7, 209

Waxhaw, 209

Waxhaws, 123, 209

HOMAS

Thomas, 18, 23, 24, 34, 55, 56, 93, 111, 112

Thomas Adams, 166, 167, 170, 195

Thomas Ambrose, 15, 22, 209

Thomas Archibald, 4, 14, 82, 92, 93, 94, 96, 97, 99, 100, 101, 102, 103, 104, 105,

Thomas Ellict, 60, 209

Thomas Hoston, 209

Thomas Houston, 4, 12, 13, 15, 18, 28, 29, 34, 37, 40, 45, 47, 209

Thomas Rogers, 36, 195

Thomas William, 123

Thomas Willis, 74, 209

THOMPSON

Thompson, 74, 92, 191

THURMAN

Thurman Bryan, 12, 15, 197, 27

TOBY

Toby, 96, 100, 101, 103, 104, 105, 108, 110, 112, 114, 211

Toby Brown, 4, 13, 65, 82, 84, 85, 86, 87, 88, 89, 90, 91, 93, 106, 117, 122, 194,

Toby Patriarch, 14, 212

TOSH

TROY

Troy, 163, 212

Troy Pearson, 141, 163, 210

TULLAHOMA

Tullahoma, 174

ULSTER

Ulster Scots, 123, 210

UNBOXED

Unboxed Past, 1, 2, 7, 209

UNBOXING

Unboxing, 4

UNITED

United States, 210, 37, 93, 120, 121, 119

UNKNOWN

Unknown, 90

Unknown Martha, 182

Unknown Notable, 183

Unknown Pictures, 210

Unknown She, 173, 175

USA

Usa Burial, 64

Usa The, 180

VALLEY

Valley, 207

VAN

Van Buren, 34, 210

VERITAS

Veritas Avenue, 43, 210

VERNA

Verna Lucretia, 60

VESTA

Vesta Emiline, 60, 210

VINA

Vina Bell, 60, 210

VIOLA

Viola, 10, 38, 42, 44, 45, 46, 47, 48, 51, 52, 55, 56, 58, 60, 68, 152, 154, 159,

Viola Tennessee, 210, 9

VIRGIE

Virgie Elizabeth, 60, 210

VIRGIL

Virgil Adams, 210

VIRGINIA

Virginia, 93, 94, 97, 98, 99, 100, 102, 104, 105, 109, 110, 111, 112,

113, 114,

Virginia Died, 210

Virginia Father, 14

Virginia She, 112

WALDEAN

Waldean Brown, 44, 202

WALDROP

Waldrop, 98, 99, 117, 205

WALICE

Walice, 50

WAR

War I, 41, 152, 153

WARREN

Warren, 30, 39, 43, 48, 49, 56, 65, 66, 67, 71, 73, 77, 82, 86, 158, 159, 177, 180,

Warren Counties, 151, 159, 161, 59

Warren County, 13, 36, 40, 41, 44, 46, 47, 48, 51, 55, 56, 57, 58, 61, 63, 65, 66, 10,

12, 13, 18, 20, 22, 23, 26, 28, 29, 34, 36, 37, 38, 41, 42, 45, 27, 63

WARS

Wars, 203

WASHINGTON

Washington County, 100

WAXHAW

Waxhaw, 209

WAXHAWS

Waxhaws, 118, 123, 209

WAYNE

Wayne County, 211, 79

WEAVER

Weaver, 50

WELCOME

Welcome, 17

WENDELL

Wendell Eaton, 154, 197

WESLEY

Wesley, 37, 44, 46, 55, 169, 195, 198

Wesley Adams, 166, 167, 169, 198

Wesley Brown, 44, 195

Wesley Chapel, 10, 146, 211

WHITE

White, 179, 182, 183, 191, 197

White County, 159, 211

WILLIAM

William, 43, 46, 48, 51, 54, 55, 56, 57, 58, 59, 61, 62, 63, 68, 83, 91, 106, 120,

William A, 177

William Andrew, 42, 46, 55, 211

William B, 167, 171, 179

William Baldwin, 38, 211

William Bill, 211

William Brown, 4, 13, 14, 46, 64, 65, 66, 67, 68, 69, 70, 71, 72, 73, 75, 76, 77, 23, 82

William Burr, 41, 211

William County, 111, 204, 102, 111, 113, 114, 115, 116

William Edward, 4, 13, 46, 47, 48, 49, 50, 51, 52, 53, 54, 56, 57, 58, 59, 60, 61, 13

William Henderson, 211

William Jr, 211, 49, 51

William L, 51

William Marshall, 74, 211

William McBrayne, 93, 117, 118, 119, 120, 121, 122, 123, 124, 125, 129, 130,

William Sr, 56, 211, 54, 59, 62

William Toby, 4, 13, 14, 65, 82, 84, 85, 86, 87, 88, 89, 90, 91, 92, 93, 96, 100,

William Zumbro, 151, 198

WILLIAMS

Williams, 46, 47, 49, 50, 51, 52, 53, 54, 56, 57, 58, 59, 60, 61, 63, 68, 192

Williams Brown, 47, 192

WILLIE

Willie Harrison, 162, 212

Willie Henderson, 212

Willie Minerva, 212

WILLIS

Willis, 74, 209

WILMA

Wilma, 154

Wilma Jean, 151, 154, 212

WILSON

Wilson, 177, 207

Wilson County, 86, 212, 83

WINSTON

Winston Knott, 5, 145, 157, 158, 159, 160, 161, 162, 163

WINTON

Winton Lynn, 192, 9

WOODVILLE

Woodville Adams, 166, 167, 172

WOOTEN

Wooten, 169, 202

WORLD

World, 110, 125, 126, 203

World War, 41, 152, 153, 212, 71

WWII

ZION

Zion Cemetery, 23, 24, 63, 202, 212

ZUMBRO

Zumbro, 5, 146, 151, 161, 189, 196, 198, 199

Zumbro Adams, 151, 199, 154

Zumbro Leta, 151

"They Have never been fogotten"

www.ingramcontent.com/pod-product-compliance
Lightning Source LLC
Chambersburg PA
CBHW020535030426
42337CB00013B/856